TOURING IN WINE COUNTRY

BAVARIA

including Baden and Württemberg

MITCHELL BEAZLEY

TOURING IN WINE COUNTRY
BAVARIA
including Baden and Württemberg

STUART PIGOTT

SERIES EDITOR
HUGH JOHNSON

Contents

**Touring in Wine Country
Bavaria**
published by Mitchell Beazley,
part of Reed Consumer Books Limited,
Michelin House, 81 Fulham Road,
London SW3 6RB
and Auckland, Melbourne, Singapore
and Toronto

First published in 1997
© Reed International Books Limited
1997
Text copyright © Reed International
Books Limited 1997
Maps copyright © Reed International
Books Limited 1997
All rights reserved

Stuart Pigott has asserted his moral
rights as author of this work.

No part of this publication may be
reproduced or used in any form by
any means, electronic or mechanical,
including photocopying, recording or
by any information storage and
retrieval system without prior
written permission of the publisher

A CIP catalogue record of this book
is available from the British Library

ISBN 1 85732 874 4

Editor: Diane Pengelly
Art Editor: Mark Richardson
Senior Art Editor: Paul Drayson
Commissioning Editor: Sue Jamieson
Executive Art Editor: Fiona Knowles
Picture Research: Claire Gouldstone
Index: Angie Hipkin
Gazetteer: Sally Chorley
Production: Christina Quigley
Cartography: Map Creation Limited
and Lovell Johns Limited

Typeset in Bembo and Gill Sans
Origination by Mandarin Offset,
Singapore
Produced by Mandarin Offset
Printed and bound in Hong Kong

Maps

Foreword

Wine, more than anything else that we eat and drink, is resonant with the sense of place. Wines are formed by the ecology of their region, their soils and climates – but what shapes their character is a broader amalgam. The whole culture of region and country, all the cross-currents of history that form its taste and individuality, determine the kind of wine its people are accustomed to.

All these factors, from the geology underlying the land, the summer rain and spring frost, to the ruling dynasties of centuries ago, form part of the elusive concept of *terroir*. The richer the region and the longer its fields have been profitably cultivated the more they stamp their personality on their produce. Why are the world's most valuable wines those from vineyards with the longest consistent records? Because every generation, every decision by their owners, has contributed to their unique qualities. (This is not to say they cannot be mishandled to produce poor wine, but that their potential is the sum of their past and present.)

You can, of course, understand wine without being aware of its origin and roots. It would be underestimating our ancestors to say that because they may never have seen a vineyard they could not appreciate and memorize its character. But we are in the happy position of being able to trace our wine directly back to the trellises, cellars and families that shaped it. It is a journey anyone can make. We can eat the food that they eat with it: become as it were honorary members of the community and culture that forms it.

No wonder wine tourism is growing exponentially. Once you have discovered the hospitality of wine growers, their desire to share (amazingly, often with their rivals too) and the way the wine community spans the globe in friendly collaboration you will want to explore it all.

If there were a wine-country hospitality league, a contest for which region puts on the best show for the visitor, nowhere in Europe would compete with Germany for the friendly welcome, the ubiquitous flowery garden or cosy fire-side, or the range of open bottles to be sampled.

Even as short a time as a decade ago wine-touring was generally limited to the Rhine and the Mosel. There were other excellent reasons for visiting the Black Forest, the valley of the Neckar in Württemberg and the Main in northern Bavaria – but wine was not high on most visitors' agendas. As for the remnant vineyards of Saxony and the Elbe in East Germany there was even less reason to go out of your way.

Yet these regions, even more than the ever-popular Rhineland, have been raising their game recently as centres of gastronomic tourism. You can eat as well in Baden or Franconia as almost anywhere in northern Europe, and match your food with wine as appetizing and savoury as almost any from France.

This book describes a vast stretch of country of rich and fascinating variety. From the almost languorous climate of Freiburg and the Kaiserstuhl, through the Black Forest with its castled crags, the luxury of Baden Baden and the dignity of Heidelburg, the bustle of Stuttgart, the rural simplicity of the Hessische Bergstrasse, the baroque grandeur of Würzburg, the oak-clad hills of the Steigerwald and on to the reborn beauties of Meissen and Dresden is a journey through layers of culture, history and climatic and topographical extremes.

Germany's *autobahns* make it appear seamless, but the wine-traveller beyond the Rhineland has the challenge of exploring well-separated, distinct and proud pockets of viticulture whose product is little known beyond their encircling woods.

Bavaria drinks its Frankenwein too enthusiastically to share much of it with the outside world. It is the same with Württemberg and its racy Rieslings, the Kaiserstuhl with its rich intense Pinots or Durbach and its stylish 'Klingelbergers'. Which only makes the journey more worthwhile. This is a pilgrimage to a new world where standard grape varieties are given a new and original twist, and vines you have never heard of make wines of genuine originality that never make it to the supermarket shelves at home.

Hugh Johnson

Introduction

Images of the Schwarzwald, or Black Forest, have been etched into the world's popular consciousness no less strongly than those of the Rhine Gorge. The region runs along the eastern side of the Rhine Valley between Lörrach and Karlsruhe and, though its natural beauty is undeniable, it is only one of many chains of forested hills and mountains in the States of Bavaria and Baden-Württemberg. The Spesart, Odenwald, Schwäbische Alb, Fränkische Wald and Steigerwald are all attractive destinations, the vineyards on favourably exposed slopes at the forest edge and along river valleys making them doubly appealing.

Many of Germany's finest wines grow in these two States and during the last decade there has been an enormous improvement in the quality of both white and red examples. Anyone not yet familiar with these wines will be amazed at the richness, depth and sophistication of the best of them, which can confidently compete with finest dry white and red wines from France, Italy or Austria.

As if that weren't enough to prompt wine tourists to start packing, the region also boasts an irresistibly high concentration of fine restaurants, including the establishments of some of the finest chefs working today. Good cooking has always been important to Badeners, so even in simple inns the standard of food is far higher than is the norm in Germany – or for that matter in many parts of France.

Although the tiny, picturesque winegrowing region of Hessische Bergstrasse is actually part of the State of Hessen, the wines and culinary pleasures it has to offer more than justify its inclusion in this guide.

The small wine regions of Saale-Unstrut and Sachsen are geographically remote from the main body of Germany's vineyards, and until the fall of the communist regime of the GDR in November 1989 they were literally

Left *The steeply-pitched roofs of Unterhambach in the Hessische Bergstrasse crowd in the valley beneath the town's vineyards.*

Top *Stone carvings of figures, faces and creatures add a curious personal touch to a rich architectural heritage.*

Wine Regions of Germany

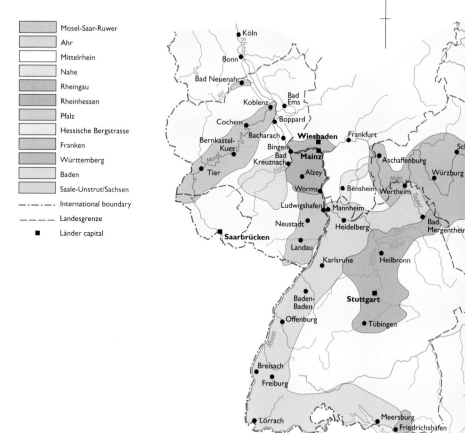

N

Mosel-Saar-Ruwer
Ahr
Mittelrhein
Nahe
Rheingau
Rheinhessen
Pfalz
Hessische Bergstrasse
Franken
Württemberg
Baden
Saale-Unstrut/Sachsen
–·–·–·– International boundary
– – – – – Landesgrenze
■ Länder capital

isolated from the rest of the country. These regions now take their rightful place in this book since they are both of great natural beauty, have a wealth of cultural heritage and are at last making some wines that deserve serious attention. Their wine culture, which goes back many centuries, is happily flowering once again.

Within the winegrowing regions covered by this guide lie several cities of enormous historic importance, whose streets contain architectural marvels at almost every turn. Würzburg and Aschaffenburg in Franken, Freiburg and Heidelberg in Baden, Stuttgart and Tübingen in Württemberg, Naumburg in Saale-Unstrut and Dresden and Meissen in Sachsen all have a great deal to offer.

From the history of these areas it is possible to learn much about the regions' contemporary wine culture. Viticultural roots penetrate as far as the early Middle Ages – often much further, and though winemaking equipment and techniques may seem to have moved into the twenty-first century, winemakers here have never lost touch with their ancient and venerable origins.

THE REGIONS

A

● Halle

● Leipzig

Unstrut

● Naumburg

furt

Elbe

Meissen

■ **Dresden**

erg

1:3 600 000

| Km 0 | | 40 | | 80 | | 120 | | 160 |
| Miles 0 | 20 | | 40 | | 60 | | 80 | 100 |

B

● Hamburg

● **Berlin**

● Hannover

● Köln

● Leipzig

● Frankfurt

● Dresden

● Stuttgart

● München

C

D

■ **München**

E

Below *This pastoral scene at Zell near Bensheim in the Hessische Bergstrasse typifies the gentle charm of Germany's 'Spring Garden'.*

F

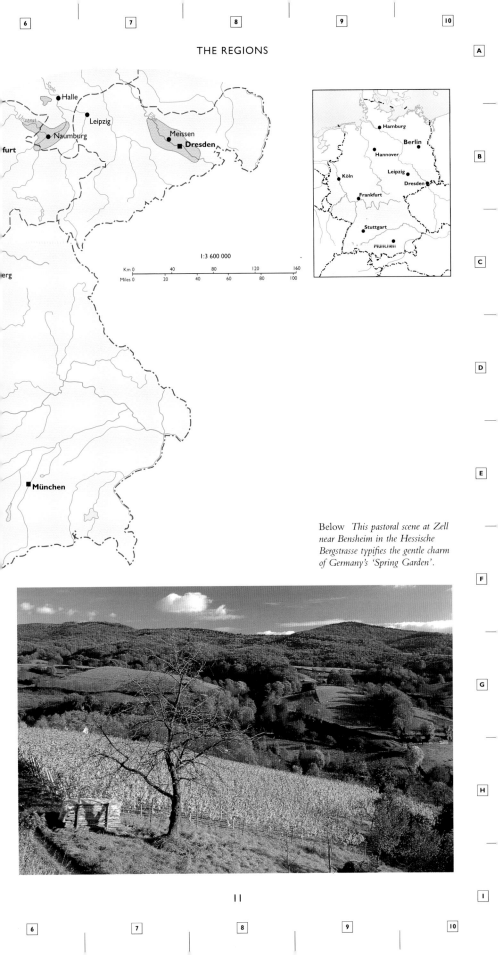

G

H

I

Landscape and climate

The Rhine's course between Lörrach and Wiesbaden forms a convenient north-south axis dividing Germany's main winegrowing regions. Those to the east can be divided into two broad zones either side of the 'wall' of the Black Forest and the Odenwald-Spesart to its north. Vineyards lying on the west of this great natural barrier – Baden (excepting Badisches Frankenland), the Hessische Bergstrasse and the western extremity of Franken – enjoy a warm temperate climate. They are protected from cold easterly airstreams by the peaks behind them; as a result the winters are seldom icy. The climate is comparable with that of the Pfalz on the opposite side of the Rhine Valley, though the most favourably exposed parts of Baden such as the Kaiserstuhl enjoy even warmer summers than the Pfalz.

In spite of nature's generosity, however, micro-climatic variations are dramatic and result in corresponding differences in quality between wines from the warmest sites and those from the coolest corners. It is no accident that early-ripening grapes such as Müller-Thurgau are planted in the less favourable areas and that the sites with auspicious micro-climates and exposure are reserved for grapes such as the Pinot family and Riesling.

East of these forested mountains the climate is more continental, having a much greater contrast between warm

Above *With almost geometric precision the land is divided – the flat lands used for agriculture and the steep south-facing slopes below the forest for viticulture. The continental climate here in Franken results in big, firm dry Rieslings, Silvaners and Müller-Thurgaus.*

summers and cold winters. Late frost in spring shortly after bud break and early frost during the harvest can cause considerable losses for winemakers. To combat this, very late-ripening grapes such as Riesling and Traminer are planted only in the very best sites, primarily in sheltered corners such as the valleys of the Main, Neckar and Elbe.

Even the less noble varieties must take advantage of whatever shelter the contours of the landscape can provide. On the plus side, hot summers make it possible to cultivate red-wine grapes over a wide area and enable substantial dry white wines to be made in good vintages.

The geology of each of these regions is far more complex than, for example, that of the Mosel-Saar-Ruwer, where a single soil type predominates. Even the 300 hectares of the tiny Sachsen region comprise granite, gneis, porphyry, loess-loam and sand soils, which account for considerable local variation in the grape varieties cultivated and in the range of wines produced. Whilst not all the styles have serious potential and a few would not be missed if they were suddenly to disappear, this diversity is an important part of the regions' appeal.

Grape varieties

Tradition and its sometime rival, fashion, can be as important as micro-climate and geology in determining which variety is cultivated where. The German workhorse grape **Müller-Thurgau** for example gained ground in all the regions covered by this guide during 1960s and 1970s as the vineyard area was expanded. In Baden, Saale-Unstrut and Sachsen it accounts for fully one third of the planted area and in Franken, nearly half. In all these regions, given moderate yields and good winemaking, the variety can yield wines with more character than the wishy-washy examples common in the Rhine and Mosel.

Almost 2,500 hectares in Württemberg are planted with the unremarkable red **Trollinge**r grape. It would be entirely possible to replant these vineyards with vines that gave more colourful and flavoursome wines: **Lemberger, Spätburgunder** (**Pinot Noir**), its close relatives **Samtrot** and **Clevner** and **Dornfelder** can all give serious red wines here. However, according to tradition, Trollinger is the Swabians' 'mothers' milk' and, beloved of innumerable Württembergers, it is unlikely to be replaced.

Below *Ruländer or Grauburgunder grapes, whose many aliases include Pinot Gris in France, Pinot Grigio in Italy and Tokay in Alsace.*

Above *Silvaner, capable of yielding great wines from first-class sites, is also the traditional workhorse grape of Baden and Franken.*
Left *A stone monument dedicated to the Klingelberger or Riesling grape stands in the vineyards of Schloss Staufenberg in Baden.*
Below *The Trollinger grape is also known as Vernatsch and as Schiava Grossa in Italy.*

In Baden most top-class wines are produced from the Pinot family: **Weissburgunder** (**Pinot Blanc**), **Ruländer/Grauburgunder** (**Pinot Gris**) and **Spätburgunder**. The first two give dry white wines with 11–14 degrees of natural alcohol, and fruit and flesh to match. Both have relatively supple acidity, Weissburgunder tending to be the more elegant wine, Grauburgunder tending towards power and lushness. The area planted with Spätburgunder, a traditional grape, has grown steadily to more than 4,000 hectares in recent years. Whilst most Baden Pinot Noirs lack structure and subtlety, recently some excellent wines have been made by the leading estates.

Only in the Ortenau area does **Riesling** play a significant role, giving wines broadly similar to those of the Pfalz but with more elegance. Hessische Bergstrasse, not far to the north, presents a similar picture.

In Franken Riesling plays a minor role since the grape will ripen fully only in top sites. Here **Silvaner** is the traditional first grape for quality wines, though much of what it yields is rustic dry wine for everyday consumption. Only in first-class vineyards does it gain an extra dimension in richness and sophistication, giving wines that Hugh Johnson has compared with Grand Cru Chablis. Sadly, during the 1960s and 1970s inferior modern vine crossings such as **Bacchus**, **Perle** and **Ortega** gained a serious foothold in Franken's vineyards, but so also did **Rieslaner**, a crossing of Riesling and Silvaner which now yields many of the region's finest and most expressive dessert wines.

In Saale-Unstrut and Sachsen large areas of vineyards are currently being replanted in order to replace the inferior varieties and poor vine material remaining from the GDR period. Of the noble grapes Riesling, **Traminer** and Weissburgunder look to have a fine future in both regions, with Grauburgunder also showing promise in Sachsen.

Vineyard classification

In the regions covered by this guide vineyard classification has never been as important a theme as it is today. This is largely because during the 18th, 19th and first half of the 20th century large areas of vineyards were few here: before the 1960s, wide expanses were planted only in the southern half of Baden. This in itself provided a kind of unplanned classification. The higher prices achieved by the wines from top sites such as the Würzburger Stein in Franken, the Ihringer Winklerberg in Baden or the Stettener Brotwasser in Württemberg made their superiority clear enough.

But in recent decades, in line with an international trend, the area under vine has been expanded and new grape varieties introduced.

Consequences have been particularly unfortunate in Bavaria, Baden and Württemberg because this expansion, actively encouraged by politicians, ran out of control. The Wine Law of 1971, which enlarged the boundaries of

Above and left *Finely manicured and precisely angled to catch the sun, rows of Riesling vines provide elegantly textured cover around Neuweier in Baden.*
Bottom left *Blue anti-bird netting adds an unfamiliar hue to the autumnal palette near Wurmling in Württemberg.*

many top vineyard sites and thus enabled famous wine-village names to be exploited by their less famous neighbours, created as many problems in Baden and Franken as it had already caused in the Mosel.

Today, the need for a clear system of vineyard classification is every bit as great here as it is elsewhere in Germany. Perhaps because Württemberg's reputation has slipped in recent years its top estates have been particularly active in exploring the classification possibilities.

The estates of Graf Adelman, Fürst zu Hohenlohe-Oehringen and Graf Neipperg have made the first move with an unofficial classification in which superior wines from the traditional grape varieties are sold under the 'Württemberg Klassisch' name.

In contrast, the Baden group of the VDP (*Verband Deutscher Prädikatsweingüter*, the German association of quality wine producers) raised eyebrows by suggesting that a classification of their regions' vineyards should exclude the great sites of Durbach simply because none of them owns vines there!

In Franken the VDP estates have been more cautious and objective in their (as yet tentative) proposals. The campaign of the Rheingau Winegrowers' Association for a legally ratified classification of their region's vineyards does have some prospect of success, however, and this is proving a powerful spur for action.

In both Saale-Unstrut and Sachsen the special character and qualities of the wines from the different sites are only just beginning to emerge. At least another five to ten years' work by the leading vintners will be necessary to define which are the important sites and which are the particular grape varieties that suit them best.

Right and left *Metal canisters have replaced wicker baskets and trailers replaced horses' carts, but on the stony granite slopes of the Durbach estate in Baden the grapes for elegant dry Rieslings and powerful Gewürztraminers are still picked by hand.*

Below *Staatsweigut Meersburg uses temperature-controlled stainless steel fermentation tanks to accentuate the delicate flavours of grapes grown in its vineyards on the banks of Bodensee (Lake Constance).*

Viticulture and winemaking

During the last 20 years most of the vineyards of Baden, Württemberg and Franken have been *Flurbereinigt* or reorganised so that each winegrower's vines stand in a small number of large parcels rather than dozens of tiny plots and each parcel of vines has a road above and below it. This sounds very positive, the aim clearly being to reduce costs by enabling winegrowers to work more easily and by facilitating mechanisation. However, the results of the huge landworks in the Kaiserstuhl in Baden show how damaging such a project can be if undertaken without sensitivity. When the first *Flurbereinigungen* here went ahead, the dozens of narrow terraces that covered each hillside were replaced by a handful of massive step-like terraces. It was not long before it became clear how impractical such large-scale contours were and now some winegrowers are calling for a complete revision that would recreate in a more practical form something like the original landscape.

Thankfully, the later *Flurbereinigungen* in these regions were undertaken with much greater respect for the landscape, soil structure and ecosystem. The only resulting problems have been associated with higher yields: reorganisation was often undertaken as a means to increase the area under vine which has lead indirectly to lower prices and marketing problems for Baden's simplest wines.

No such problems have beset the former GDR, however, where replanting in recent decades was primarily designed to allow normal tractors to be used in cultivation.

Spaces up to three metres wide were introduced between rows: practical for tractors but a catastrophic move as far as the quality of the harvest was concerned. On paper the yields per hectare look low, which normally suggests a high-quality product, but the wines from such vineyards taste thin and characterless as each vine has to support too many bunches and much of its energy is directed into making leaves and stems. In an effort to redress this imbalance, substantial replanting is currently under way in the Saale-Unstrut and Sachsen.

White-winemaking in all these regions has followed the same path during the last decades: away from wooden casks and lengthy barrel ageing and towards stainless steel, cool fermentations and early bottling. Many of the best dry white wines are now made in stainless steel in accordance with modern ideas. Updating techniques in this way is fine until the point is reached at which the technology, rather than the experience and instinct of the cellarmaster, starts to dictate what happens to the young wines. Thankfully many winemakers have realised that the trend was moving too far in the direction of neutral wines and superficial fruit. Now there is a reversion towards the use of wood for top-quality white wines.

And the reds? The leading estates of Baden and Württemberg have made enormous advances during recent years. Today the top-quality red wines are fermented on the skins for around two weeks, undergo full malolactic fermentation and are matured in small new-oak casks for between one and two years just as the great red wines of Burgundy and Bordeaux are. As these methods become more widely adopted and winemakers gain experience and confidence, we can look forward to further improvements.

Above *Careful calculation of the optimum angle for each row has resulted in complex geometric patterns on the slopes of Schloss Staufen.*

Right *Karl Heinz Johner among the new-oak barriques in his cellar in Bischoffingen, Baden.* Far right *The steep granite slopes of Durbach produce Baden's finest Rieslings.*

Visiting wine estates

Winemakers in Germany as everywhere usually love to talk about their wines and taste them with interested visitors. When planning a trip however it is worth remembering that, with the exception of the large estates of Würzburg and the cooperatives of Baden, most of the best wines are produced by small, family-run estates. If at all possible do try to ring to make appointments in advance otherwise you may find that nobody is there to receive you. When travelling bear in mind that turning up late for an appointment can be worse than not making one at all. A short call to report delays is always appreciated. Most of the producers featured in this guide speak English.

Harvest time, which generally begins in the last days of September and extends well into October, is one of great stress for winegrowers. During this period producers may still receive visitors but will be able to them spare less time and will probably be less relaxed than usual!

At the larger estates and cooperatives which have facilities for receiving visitors without appointments there is no need to buy anything, although some purchase will be appreciated. At smaller estates it is discourteous to take up a winegrower's time and not take something away with you.

Cuisine

Above *Black Forest ham, rye bread and dry Grauburgunder: a simple but tempting combination whose popularity has endured for centuries.*

Food, just like wine, reflects the history and culture of those who produce and consume it. The contrasting cuisines of regions covered by this guide say a great deal about their differing cultures and histories.

Baden, together with Alsace and the German-speaking part of Switzerland, belong to the Allemagnic region whose culture is strongly influenced by France. The style here is definitely country cooking rather than the self-conscious Grand Cuisine of Paris or Lyon, but it is of a particularly rich and refined kind. For ordinary Badeners, eating at a good restaurant is not unusual: differing incomes influence the frequency with which such excursions are made but not the general attitude to good food. As a result, standards are high and there are also dozens of top-class restaurants. To see this in perspective, consider the spa town of Baiersbronn situated in the Black Forest. It has 16,000 inhabitants and its restaurants, which include one of Germany's greatest, the Schwarzwaldstube of Harald Wohlfahrt, have earned among them six Michelin stars. Even the nation's capital Berlin, with 3.5 million inhabitants, cannot muster this number of Michelin stars.

Not surprisingly given the vast areas of forest in Baden the game, the venison in particular, is very good indeed. Traditionally it is served with irregularly shaped *Spätzle* noodles. The forests also yield an abundant crop of wild mushrooms during summer and early autumn. White

Right *Nuts and dried fruits, essential ingredients in many traditional sweetmeats, on display in Reutlingen market.*

Below *Few of the older high streets are without pieces of original craftsmanship such as this eye-catching butchers' sign from Reutlingen, Württemberg.*

asparagus is a speciality, particularly in the Kaiserstuhl where it is cultivated on the plain. Cherry orchards in the hills provide fruit for succulent jams and for Schnapps that is frequently superior to the heavily commercialised eaux-de-vie of neighbouring Alsace.

In Württemberg too the cooking tends to be rich and substantial, the general standard far superior to that tailored to tourists in the Mosel or Mittelrhein. There is a good number of high-class restaurants, including the superb Friedrichsruhe of Lothar Eiermann. Franken also has a great restaurant, Andreas Schmitt's Schweizer Stuben, but it is something of a gastronomic oasis. Culinary traditions here are extremely rustic. The sausage reigns supreme, portions are large and flavours hearty rather than fine.

Just as the winemakers of Saale-Unstrut and Sachsen are rediscovering their viticultural traditions, so the local chefs and innkeepers are finding their own style of cooking. It is already possible to eat very well, but do not expect anything grand. Proprietors, keen to win over the local inhabitants, tend to be wary of extravagant or complex dishes.

How to use this guide

Above *Albrechtsburg Castle, designed by Arnold von Westfalen in the early 15th century, overlooks the River Elbe near Meissen and marks the town's original site. The castle is one of the finest civic examples of the late-Gothic style.*

This guide, which covers the eastern winegrowing regions in Germany, from Baden to the northeastern extremity of Sachsen and Saale-Unstrut, is designed to help those travellers who wish to make their own plans and write their own itineraries as well as those who want to be guided each step of the way.

A route or a series of routes is described through the heart of each wine region. Wine sites, towns and villages along the route are included – as well as one or two whose lack of drinkable product is compensated by a special richness of history or culture. The best producers in each area are described, as are local hotels, restaurants and places of interest.

If you decide to follow one of the suggested routes and you visit the estates mentioned, the trip will take up the better part of a day (depending on your exact starting point). If you have leisure to explore in more detail, the maps are designed to enable all the important vineyards along the path to be identified. The most convenient starting points

for regional tours are Lörrach for the southern half of
Baden; Stuttgart for Württemberg and the northern half of
Baden; Frankfurt for Hessische Bergstrasse and Franken,
and Dresden for the Saale-Unstrut and Sachsen.

WINE PRODUCERS AND WHERE TO BUY WINE

Thumb-nail sketches of producers give an overview of the
important estates. In the wine regions east of the Rhine the
best places to buy wine are almost always at the estates
themselves. Good wine stores are, sadly, rare. Extensive
selections of fine German wines can be found at Weinland-
Keiler in Neu-Isenburg (close to Frankfurt) and Munich,
Käfer in Munich, and Feinkost Böhm in Stuttgart.

RESTAURANTS

Suggestions for eating out focus on the best restaurants and
on moderately-priced places with good rustic food. It
would be a shame to visit the regions where some of
Europe's finest restaurants are located, however, and not
sample at least one of the best. At such places you should
allow DM100–150 for a small menu or up to DM200 for
a large one (excluding wine etc). This is certainly not
cheap, but compared to the prices charged at the great
restaurants of France, these are modest. You may be able to
secure a table for lunch at relatively short notice but if you
want to be sure of a table for dinner, try to book two or
three months in advance.

In Baden the general standard of cooking is remarkably
high and you may well chance upon unlisted establishments
that are good. In other regions this is less likely. The
quality of top restaurants in the former-GDR Saale-Unstrut
and Sachsen should not be underestimated, but
recommendations should be followed closely.

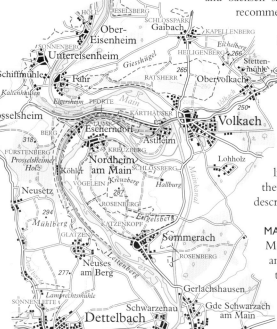

HOTELS

Hotel recommendations in this
guide are made using criteria
similar to those which govern
the selection of restaurants.

PLACES OF INTEREST

The most important historical
and architectural monuments are
listed separately. In places where
they are particularly abundant they are
described in the main text.

MAPS
Maps illustrate each of the regions
and locate the suggested wine routes,
taking in the most important
villages and vineyards. They give
enough detail to allow fuller
exploration if there is time.

Baden

Although both the Pfalz and Rheinhessen have more vineyards and produce more wine than Baden, Baden's vineyards are scattered over a far wider area than those of other German wine regions. In some instances distances between vineyards are over 400 kilometres. Contrasts among the area's many beautiful landscapes are also dramatic: between Lake Constance with its views of alpine peaks on one hand and the twisting Tauber Valley on the other; the rolling hills around Heidelberg and the mass of the Kaiserstuhl towering above the Rhine Valley. Concomitant with the extremes of scenery are, or course, dramatic variations in climate and soil.

In spite of these variations, the wines of Baden all bear a family resemblance. This is as a result of a common winemaking tradition and of the fact that the same noble grape varieties, particularly those of the Pinot family (Weissburgunder, Grauburgunder and Spätburgunder) are to be found throughout the region.

In many respects this area is as strongly linked to Alsace and the northern, German-speaking part of Switzerland as it is to the rest of Germany and there are strong parallels between the vine-growing and winemaking traditions of all three. One of Baden's leading vintners once half-jokingly suggested that if these parts of Germany, France and Switzerland could form their own country it would make a good deal of sense. However, during recent decades the areas' produce has diverged somewhat and Baden has developed its own set of distinctive wine styles.

In volume terms its most important product is dry Müller-Thurgau which accounts for more than a third of the region's wines. This grape is hardly found in Alsace and plays only a minor role in Switzerland, but in less favoured vineyards throughout Baden it is capable of giving pleasant light dry wines that are not too acidic. Ruländer and

Left *Early-18th-century Brüchsal Castle has been reconstructed since its total destruction in 1945.*

Top *Bodensee or Lake Constance offers opportunities for all kinds of leisure activities and excursions.*

Grauburgunder are the dominant producers of high-quality white wines. Although the varieties are in fact the same vine as the Tokay Pinot Gris of Alsace, both its German incarnations are completely different. Ruländer is sweeter and heavier than its Alsatian cousin while Grauburgunder is crisper and less opulent. Baden's Weissburgunders taste like discreet and elegant versions of its Grauburgunders rather than resembling Alsace Pinot Blancs.

During the last decade the area planted with the Spätburgunder grape variety in Baden has grown rapidly to 4,250 hectares, making the region a red-wine producer of considerably more importance than either Alsace or northern Switzerland. This increased importance related to quality as well as volume. Baden's new-style oak-aged Spätburgunders have been attracting favourable opinion right around the globe in recent years.

Although Riesling is not usually associated with Baden, more than 1,000 hectares in the region are now planted with the vine. At least in the Ortenau the results are regularly impressive, having more in common with the Rieslings of the Pfalz than with those of Alsace. Specialities such as aromatic Gewürztraminer, Muskateller and Scheurebe also deserve to be taken seriously. The combination of these vinous riches, the cuisine of the region's many fine restaurants and dramatic views of the Black Forest is indeed hard to resist.

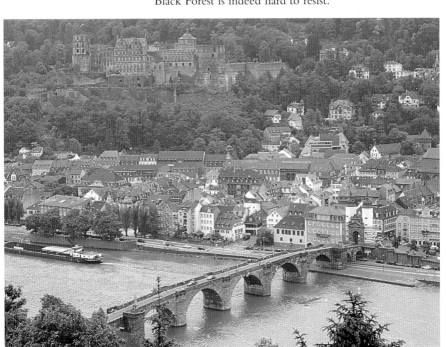

Above *The Alte or Karl-Theodor Brücke (bridge) spans the Neckar below Heidelberg, seat of Germany's most famous university since 1386.*

Parts of the Schloss on the hill date from the 14th century: subsequent alterations represent virtually every architectural period since.

**BODENSEE
AND SINGEN**

RECOMMENDED PRODUCERS

Aufricht
Weinkundeweg 8
D 88709 Meersburg
Tel: (07532) 6123
Robert and Manfred Aufricht make
clean, fruity dry whites, including a
classic Bodensee Müller-Thurgau with
the help of Herbert Senft,
winemaker for the Markgraf von
Baden estate. Appointment
recommended.
Thomas Geiger
Baitenhauser Strasse 3a
D 88709 Meersburg-Riedetsweiler
Tel: (07532) 9856
Elegant, crisp Spätburgunder
Weissherbst (Pinot Noir rosé) is the
speciality. Good dry whites too. By
appointment only.
**Markgraf von Baden
(Bodensee)**
Schloss Salem, D 88682
Tel: (07553) 81271
Winemaker Herbert Senft is
responsible for the lively dry Müller-
Thurgaus and elegant Spätburgunder
rosés at this large estate.
Appointment essential weekends.
Staatsweingut Meersburg
Seminarstrasse 6
D 88709 Meersburg
Tel: (07532) 356
When on form, Germany's oldest
state winery can make Bodensee's
best wines but recently its
performance has been erratic.
Appointment recommended.

BODENSEE AND SINGEN

With its verdant hills, picturesque old towns and views of
distant alpine peaks the Bodensee, or Lake Constance, is a
popular tourist destination. The white and rosé wines from
the 350 hectares of vineyards in this most southerly part of
Baden are so popular with tourists that little of it finds its
way to other parts of Germany, let alone to export markets.
The result is that the wines remain little known outside the
area and thus there are few incentives for producers to
strive for top quality. This is disappointing since, though
the region could hardly be more beautiful the wines could
certainly bear some improvement.

Driving from Munich you arrive in the region on the
A96 *Autobahn* which brings you to the town of Lindau im
Bodensee, literally Lindau in Lake Constance. The old
town occupies a small island just under a kilometre in
length. Its streets are narrow and cobbled (do not take the
car; flat shoes are also a good idea), it is surrounded by
towers from ancient fortifications and gardens, and the
harbour gives magnificent views of the Alps. Not
surprisingly it is one of the region's major tourist
attractions.

Lindau's vineyards and those of the pretty towns of
Wasserburg and Nonnenhorn to its west (see map page 68)
are technically part of Franken since they belong to the state
of Bavaria. The dry whites (mainly Müller-Thurgau) can be
pleasantly refreshing but are of no great consequence. The
climate in which the grapes are grown is affected by the
cooling influence of the Bregenzer Wald peaks just over the
border in Austria. However, in this area the quality of the
apple harvest is far superior to that of the grapes. Local fruit
farmers have concentrated on traditional varieties rather than
succumbing to the trend for flavourless big croppers such as

HOTELS

Adler
See Restaurants.

Bad Schachen
D 88131 Lindau-Bad Schachen
Tel: (08382) 2980
In a beautiful lakeside park this fine
spa hotel is full of the charm of
bygone days. Indoor and outdoor
swimming pools and tennis courts.

Bayerischer Hof
Seepromenade, D 88131 Lindau
Tel: (08382) 9150
Very comfortable, perfectly
positioned – and prices to match.
Closed mid- November until Easter.

Berghotel Baader
See Restaurants.

Drei Stuben
See Restaurants.

Seehotel Siber
See Restaurants.

Seewirt (zum Engel)
Seestrasse 15, D 88149 Nonnenhorn
Tel: (08382) 89142
Family-run, on lakeside, a café
terrace under chestnut trees. Reliable
regional cooking (fish). Pleasant,
reasonably comfortable rooms.

Steigenberger Inselhotel
Auf der Insel 1, D 78462 Konstanz
Tel: (07531) 1250
In a former abbey on an island in
Lake Constance. Lovely terrace; less
exciting restaurant.

Villino
Hoyerberg 34
D 88131 Lindau-Hoyren
Tel: (08382) 93450
Small, just outside Lindau. A beautiful
terrace; good Italian restaurant.

Top *Lindau's old streets were built
in prosperous times when the island
was an important trading centre.*
Left *A tranquil view from Birnau
on the Überlinger See.*

Above *The stepped gable of a
Burgher's house in Meersburg. The
town is described as 'am' or by
Bodensee rather than 'im' or in like
Lindau, with its island setting.*

31

Right *Meersburg, on the shores of Germany's own 'Riviera', draws many German holidaymakers.* Below right *Attractive quays along the lakeshore (Seeufer) offer all kinds of diversions.*

RESTAURANTS

Hotel Adler
Oberdorfer Strasse 11
D 88085 Langenargen
Tel: (07543) 3090
Rudolf Karr's small hotel and excellent restaurant lie between Lindau and Friedrichshafen. Local fish is the speciality. Excellent wine list.

Berghotel Baader
Salemer Strasse 5
D 88633 Heiligenberg
Tel: (07554) 303
Small hotel and fine restaurant in hills behind Salem. Sophisticated cooking and generous portions make prices seem reasonable.

Brauereigasthof Krone
Bärenplatz 7, D 88069 Tettnang
Tel: (07542) 7452
Traditional Swabian inn: good rustic cooking, local wines and home-brewed beer. Simple, pleasant rooms.

Restaurant and Hotel Drei Stuben
Kirchstrasse 7, D 88709 Meersburg
Tel: (07532) 6019
Star cook Stefan Marquard presents superb modern cuisine with Italian touches. Beautifully restored half-timbered house with modern rooms. Fair prices. Reservation essential.

Hoyerberg Schlössle
Hoyerberg 64 (auf dem Hoyerberg)
D 88131 Lindau-Hoyren
Tel: (08382) 25295
Friedbert Lang's classic German-French cooking and a huge range of French wines plus breathtaking views of the lake and Alps from the terrace. Reservation essential.

Schachener Hof
Schachener Strasse 76
D 88131 Lindau-Bad Schachen
Tel: (08382) 3116
Swabian Thomas Kraus' cooking is well prepared and precisely cooked. Moderate prices and friendly service.

Seehotel Siber
Seestrasse 25, D 78464 Konstanz
Tel: (07531) 63044
Chef Bertold Siber's modern reinterpretation of classic cuisine, good Bodensee wines and ravishing views can all be found in this restored Art Nouveau villa. Hotel rooms are stylish and elegant but both they and the restaurant are expensive. Reservation essential.

Villino
See Hotels.

Golden Delicious. Fruit brandies are a speciality and frequently outclass the Alsace eaux de vie.

Following the B31 west you pass more patches of vines close to Kressbronn. These, somewhat confusingly, belong to Württemberg (*see* map page 68) but once again their wines are relatively unimportant in terms of both quantity and quality. Pass through the town of Friedrichshafen (unless you want to take the ferry to Romanshorn on the Swiss side of the lake). The top vineyards of the area lie on the south-facing slopes arising from the bank of the lake between Kirchberg and Birnau. Their high altitude – between 400 and 500 metres above sea level – makes this the coolest part of Baden. The combination of ideal exposure and the virtual absence of extreme heat makes it possible to grow fresh and delicate dry white and rosé wines. The morning fogs in late summer and autumn make red wine production difficult but the Spätburgunder (Pinot Noir) rosé can be fine.

The old town of Meersburg with its two castles perched on a hilltop directly overlooking the lake is arguably even more beautiful than Lindau. Its Altes Schloss is the oldest castle in Germany, dating back to 630, but the baroque Neues Schloss standing above the steep Rieschen vineyard is the sight which imprints itself on most visitors' minds.

Aufricht is the area's best producer, followed by Thomas Geiger and the erratic Staatsweingut. From here it is a short drive to Birnau, whose baroque church stands majestically above the vineyards along the lakeside.

The town of Singen 32 kilometres to the west of the lake, is renowned for its Olgaberg vineyard which, climbing to an

PLACES OF INTEREST

Birnau
The fine rococo pilgrimage church of Birnau (1750) with magnificent ceiling painting by Gottfried Goetz is set close to the lakeside. At the neighbouring Markgraf von Baden estate you can taste the wines or enjoy a light meal.

Konstanz
The beautiful old town of Konstanz is centred around the Münster with its magnificent western tower and remarkable medieval frescos. Begun in the mid-11th century building was completed in the late-17th century. The Renaissance Rathaus is also impressive as is the 14th-century Kaufhaus on the harbour.

Mainau
With its castle and botanic garden this small island in Lake Constance is a popular day-trip destination. Do not expect peace and quiet.

Meersburg
The old town of Meersburg is often overrun by tourists in fine weather. The Altes Schloss dates back to the 7th century but much of the town from the 16th and early-17th centuries. The imposing Neues Schloss is a classic example of southern German baroque. The neighbouring former seminary has an astonishing rococo chapel. There is a wealth of 16th- to 18th-century half-timbered houses and magnificent views over the lake to the Alps beyond – except when there is fog!

Oberuhldingen
The Pfahlbauten open-air museum centres around the excavated remains of an ancient fishing village.

Reichenau
The largest island in the Bodensee is better known for its vegetable gardens than its (unexceptional) wines. One of the few secluded spots in these parts.

Salem
Half-an-hour's drive from Meersburg lies the former Cistercian monastery of Salem. Most of the huge complex of buildings dates from the decades following its destruction by the French in 1697. Today it is home to the family of the Markgraf von Baden and an exclusive boarding school.

FESTIVALS

Bregenz, Austria
Each year Bregenz, just over the border, stages a series of excellent outdoor classic concerts during July and August. The location directly on the bank of Lake Constance makes them extremely popular and tickets should be obtained well in advance.

altitude of 560 metres on the steep slopes of the Hohentwiel, is the highest in Germany. The medieval fortress with its 16th-century Schloss crowns the Hohentwiel: this and the old town below it are as impressive as some of the minerally Weissburgunder wines (see Staatsweingut Meersburg) produced here.

MARKGRÄFLERLAND

RECOMMENDED PRODUCERS

Blankenhorn
Baslerstrasse 2, D 79418 Schliengen
Tel: (07635) 1092
Resolute Rosemarie Blankenhorn's
clean dry whites and reds are
consistently good. Appointment
essential at weekends.

**Winzergenossenschaft
Britzingen**
Markgräfler Strasse 25
D 79379 Britzingen
Tel: (07631) 4011
Elegant dry Weissburgunder and
Grauburgunder. Avoid the bizarre
new-oak-aged dessert wines. Closed
Saturday afternoons and Sundays.

Hermann Dörflinger
Mühlenstrasse 7, D 79379 Mülheim
Tel: (07631) 2207
Some of the Markgräflerland's best
Gutedel and a wide range of other
good dry whites. Reds less interesting
– rather old-fashioned. Appointment
recommended; closed Sundays.

Lämmlin-Schindler
Mülheimer Strasse 4
D 79418 Mauchen
Tel: (07635) 440
Extremely subtle and elegant organic
dry whites and reds – particularly
good Weissburgunder. Appointment
essential at weekends.

Schlossgut Idstein
Im Schloss, D 79588 Idstein
Tel: (07628) 1284
Clean, modern-style dry Gutedel and
Weissburgunder. Fruity Spätburgunder
reds but must be drunk young.
Appointment essential at weekends.

Hartmut Schlumberger
Weinstrasse 19, D 79295 Laufen
Tel: (07634) 8992
Best known for dry Weissburgunder
but Scheurebe, Gewürztraminer with
natural sweetness and fruit brandies
also good. Appointment essential at
weekends.

HOTELS

Alte Post
An der B 3, D 79379 Mülheim
Tel: (07631) 5522
Pleasant, small; fine restaurant serves
regional and vegetarian dishes. Very
good wine list. Moderate prices.

Villa Erben
Hünerbergweg 26, D 79539 Lörrach
Tel: (07621) 2066
Small, comfortable, set in a lovely
park. Quiet and moderately priced.

*Ruins of the once-substantial Burg,
sacked during the 17th century,
overlook the vineyards of Staufen.*

MARKGRÄFLERLAND

The hills of the Markgräflerland between the outskirts of Basel on the Swiss-German border and the southern edge of Freiburg contribute to one of the most charming parts of Baden. Their proximity to Switzerland has had a strong influence on the area's winegrowing traditions.

Gutedel, or Chasselas, was introduced from Switzerland in 1780 and is now the dominant grape variety accounting for half of the area's vineyard. Here it gives a much fresher, cleaner wine than further south due to its vinification in a German style (in Switzerland nearly all white wines undergo malolactic fermentation, which makes them softer and less fruity than German whites). Well made Gutedel is an ideal summer wine, light and crisp enough to be refreshing without being too tart. A good example ought to have a slightly nutty character.

The vineyards on the southern and eastern faces of the rolling hills generally have limestone soils. These are as well suited to the Pinot family – Weissburgunder, Grauburgunder, Spätburgunder and more recently Chardonnay – as they are ill-suited to Riesling. Here they give medium-bodied wines with fresh-fruit aromas, wines which have a lighter touch than those of the Kaiserstuhl to the immediate north. Even with 13.5 degrees of natural alcohol there is rarely a suggestion of heaviness. While

Above *A rampant lion, leaping deer and golden cornucopia of vines announce a small guesthouse in Staufen.*

RESTAURANTS

Hirschen
Hauptstrasse 69, D 79295 Sulzburg
Tel: (07634) 8208
Hans-Paul Steiner combines delicately flavoured *haut cuisine* with the very best local ingredients. Expensive; reservation essential.

Inzlinger Wasserschloss
Riehenstrasse 5, D 79594 Inzlingen
Tel: (07621) 47057
Excellent meat dishes and good ocean fish served in Inzlingen's moated castle. Fairly expensive food; moderately priced rooms.

Stucki
Bruderholzallee 42, CH 4000 Basel
Tel: (061) 3618222
Hans Stucki's cuisine is marked by great simplicity and unbeatable purity of flavour. Cheese, dessert and wine list all astonishing. Expensive, but not unreasonable. Reservation essential.

La Vigna
Weinstrasse 7, D 79295 Laufen
Tel: (07634) 8014
Excellent Italian restaurant run by purist chef Antonio Esposito.

Zum Adler
Hauptstrasse 139
D 79576 Weil am Rhine
Tel: (07621) 75055
Light, sophisticated cooking at moderate prices.

PLACES OF INTEREST

Badenweiler
The ruins of the Roman baths in the Spa park of Badenweiler date from the 1st century AD.

Staufen
Staufen, with noteworthy Renaissance Rathaus and Marktbrunnen fountain, lies where the Münstertal Valley enters that of the Rhine.

Sulzburg
The austere Romanesque St Cyriakskirche is a rare survivor from this period in the region.

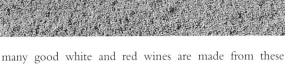

many good white and red wines are made from these grapes here few have the concentration, power or elegance of the best from further north in Baden.

Follow the A5 *Autobahn* north from Basel and take the Effringen-Kirchen exit, then follow the signs to Istein for Schloss Istein, the best producer in the southern part of the Markgräflerland. The vineyards here are widely scattered between fields and orchards and it is not until you reach the environs of Schliengen, 12 kilometres further north (follow the small road alongside the *Autobahn*) that vines begin to dominate the landscape. Schliengen is home to the Blankenhorn estate and neighbouring Mauchen to the rising star of the Markgräflerland, Lämmlin-Schindler. A few kilometres further north lies the attractive old town of Mülheim and the well known Hermann Dörflinger estate. Today the estate faces some tough competition from the cooperative of Mülheim's suburb Britzingen and from Hartmut Schlumberger in the nearby village of Laufen.

Staufen may not boast any important wine producers but it is one of the most beautiful small towns in the region. Standing beneath its ruined Schloss on the peak of the Schlossberg it has many fine half-timbered houses, an imposing Renaissance Rathaus and the 18th-century Löwen Gasthaus. Legend has it that Faust, whose life story formed the basis of Goethe's masterpiece, worked on the alchemical production of gold here. Not only did his experiments prove fruitless but they also cost him his life: he is supposed to have been killed in an explosion when the last of them went wrong.

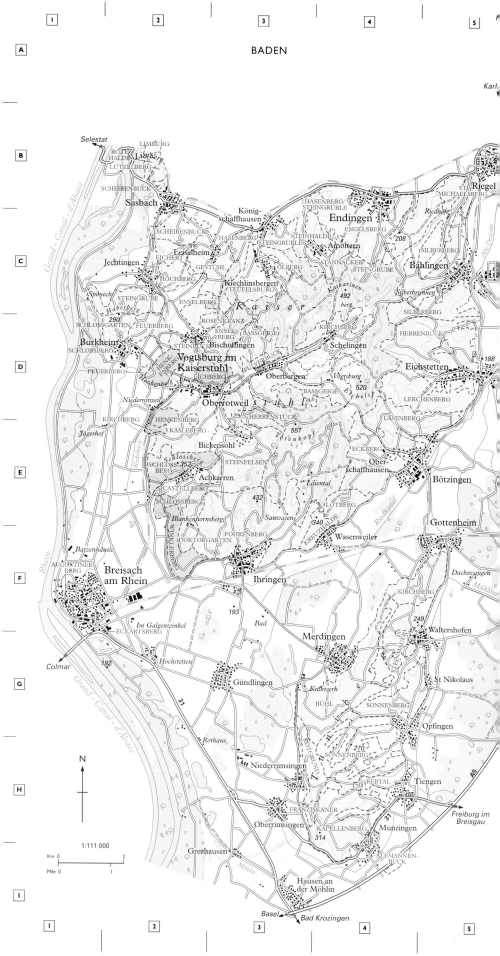

BADEN

Karl.

N
1:111 000

Km 0 2
Mile 0 I

Baden: Kaiserstuhl and Tuniberg

<u>EICHBERG</u> Einzellage

☐ First-class vineyard

☐ Other vineyard

☐ Woods

Contour interval 50 metres

Wine route

Below Pickers begin work on the slopes of the Kaiserstuhl near Vogtsburg while early morning mist still hangs over the vineyard.

KAISERSTUHL AND TUNIBERG

Mention Baden to anyone familiar with German wines and it is usually an image of the Kaiserstuhl or of its wines that most readily springs to mind. This is not surprising, since not only do the region's most dramatic vineyards lie around the 'Emperor's Throne', but also a large percentage of the best Baden wines grow here. The slogan of Baden's wine promotion, 'von der Sonne verwöhnt', or 'spoiled by the sun', certainly applies fully to these vineyards. During the summer you can actually watch as storms pass around the Kaiserstuhl, its vineyards remaining bathed in sunshine while rain falls on all sides.

The extinct volcano is now only a fraction of the height it was when, 30 million years ago, it spewed lava across the lower part of the Rhine rift valley but the Kaiserstuhl still towers above the surrounding country and is visible from a large part of Alsace on the other side of the Rhine. The best-exposed slopes on its southwestern side are among the steepest vineyards in the southern half of Germany and enjoy a warmer micro-climate than anywhere in the country. This, combined with the slopes' volcanic tuffa soils, is a recipe for dry whites wines which are rich and powerful but at the same time suave and silky. It is a poor

KAISERSTUHL AND TUNIBERG

RECOMMENDED PRODUCERS

Winzergenossenschaft Achkarren
Schlossbergstrasse 2
D 79235 Achkarren
Tel: (07662) 93040
True to an old-fashioned winemaking style, this co-op maintains a good standard with its rich dry Grauburgunder and fresh Muskateller. Closed Saturday afternoons and Sundays.

Bercher
Mittelstadt 13, D 79235 Burkheim
Tel: (07662) 212
The high points of Rainer and Eckhardt Bercher's wide range are rich dry Weissburgunders and Grauburgunders, the Kaiserstuhl's best Rieslings and Muskatellers and powerful silky Spätburgunder reds. By appointment only.

Winzergenossenschaft Bötzingen
Hauptstrasse 13, D 79268 Bötzingen
Tel: (07663) 93060
This co-op consistently produces succulently fruity dry Weissburgunder. Closed Saturday afternoons and Sundays.

Dr Heger
Bachenstrasse 19, D 79241 Ihringen
Tel: (07668) 205
Joachim Heger makes arguably the best dry Grauburgunder in Germany His Spätburgunder reds need time to give their best but are remarkably concentrated. Also very good Weissburgunder, Chardonnay and Muskateller. By appointment only.

Karl H Johner
Gartenstrasse 20
D 79235 Bischoffingen
Tel: (079235) 6041
Karl Heinz Johner's seductively perfumed, silky Spätburgunder reds and rich but precisely balanced Weissburgunders still lead the way for new-oak-aged wines. His top wines are sold as 'SJ' reserve. By appointment only.

Kalkbödele
Enggasse 21
D 79291 Merdingen
Tel: (07668) 711113
Tobias Burtsche runs the Tuniberg's best estate. Good Spätburgunder reds, less interesting dry whites. Appointment essential at weekends.

Winzergenossenschaft Königschaffhausen
Kiechlinsberger Strasse 2
D 79346 Königschaffhausen
Tel: (07642) 1003
With winemaker Helmut Staiblin, director Willi Merkle makes powerful

vintage when Weissburgunder or Grauburgunder from its top sites does not achieve 13 degrees of natural alcohol.

Most of the vineyards are planted on loess soils, soils formed from a yellowish powder brought by winds from Central Asia tens of thousands of years ago. Some layers many metres thick are visible where large terraces were cut into the hillsides during the *Fluerbereinigung*, or vineyard reorganisation, during the 1970s and 80s. This soil also covers the chalk outcrop that forms the nearby Tuniberg range of hills. These soils give white wines with more fruit and less minerally character or power than those from the volcanic tuffa.

Whichever the soil type, the Pinot family of grapes accounts for a good two thirds of all plantings. Silvaner is the traditional grape for everyday drinking whites but its wines never match good Weissburgunders or Grauburgunders.

Nowhere in Germany has the red wine revolution of recent years been more dramatic than in the Kaiserstuhl and Tuniberg areas. The first experiments with ageing Spätburgunder (Pinot Noir) red wines in new oak casks

during the early 1980s yielded some disastrous results but the leading winemakers learned very quickly from their mistakes. Today Bercher, Dr Heger and Karl H Johner are making Spätburgunder reds that can stand comparison with village and lighter Premier Cru wines from Burgundy's Cote d'Or. A handful of others producers are not far behind. French Master of Wine Olivier Humbrecht of Domaine Zind Humbrecht in Alsace recently described the wines as 'more impressive than the Oregon Pinot Noirs which have caused so much excitement'.

The Kaiserstuhl is best approached from the Riegel exit of the A5 *Autobahn* just north of Freiburg. Follow the road to Endingen where the estate of Reinhold and Cornelia Schneider, founded only in 1981, makes the best wines on this side of the Kaiserstuhl. The cooperative of the next village, Königsschaffhausen, has an excellent reputation for its powerful, oaky Spätburgunder red wines and smoky dry Grauburgunders. Today their principal challenger among the area's cooperatives is that of Sasbach, which makes opulent dry Weissburgunder and rich, silky Spätburgunder from vineyards clinging to the volcanic outcrop of the

new-oak-aged Spätburgunder reds and dry Grauburgunder whites. Also good Auslese, BA and Eiswein dessert wines. Closed Saturday afternoons and Sundays.

Gebrüder Müller
Richard-Müller-Strasse 5
D 79206 Breisach
Tel: (07667) 511
In 1990 Peter Bercher, brother of the Burkheim Berchers, built new cellars and appointed a new winemaker Joachim Lang. Quality has improved steadily. Good Spätburgunder and Cabernet-Merlot reds. Appointment recommended.

Salwey
Hauptstrasse 2, D 79235 Oberrotweil
Tel: (07662) 384
Wolf-Dietrich Salwey makes a wide range of fine dry whites (including excellent Ruländer from the Oberrotweiler Eichberg), superb rosé from the Breisgau, interesting reds plus a huge selection of first-class fruit brandies. Appointment recommended; closed Sundays.

Winzergenossenschaft Sasbach
Jechtinger Strasse 26
D 79361 Sasbach
Tel: (07642) 1044
Quality at this co-op can be variable but is rightly renowned for its opulent dry Weissburgunder and supple Spätburgunder reds. Closed Saturday afternoons and Sundays.

Reinhold and Cornelia Schneider
Königschaffhauser Strasse 2
D 79346 Endingen
Tel: (07642) 5278
Since 1982 the Schneiders have established a good reputation for

Above *Red and white wines mature in the extensive barrique cellar at Dr Heger in Ihringen.* Left *Terraced vineyards scale the Kaiserstuhl above Oberbergen.*

their fresh dry Weissburgunder, Grauburgunder and Müller-Thurgau whites. By appointment only; closed Sundays.

Franz Keller/Schwarzer Adler
Badbergstrasse 23
D 79235 Oberbergen
Tel: (07662) 93300
Fritz Keller runs not only the family's wine estate but also its wine import company (with an amazing range of French wines) and the Schwarzer Adler restaurant and hotel. The best of his own production are the new-oak-aged Weissburgunders, particularly the 'S' bottlings, and the Spätburgunder reds. Appointment essential at weekends for tastings, or take advantage of the good wine prices in the restaurant. The first-class cuisine is a mix of classic French and regional cooking.

Stigler
Bachenstrasse 29, D 79241 Ihringen
Tel: (07668) 297
The Stigler family's traditional-style dry Weissburgunder, Grauburgunder and Spätburgunder Weissherbst from the great Winklerberg site of Ihringen need time to show their best. Also good 'Blanc de Noir' Sekt. Appointment recommended.

 HOTELS

Am Münster
Münsterbergstrasse 23
D 79206 Breisach
Tel: (07667) 8380
Comfortable, modern, in town centre with a wonderful view across the Rhine Plain. Moderate prices.

Schwarzer Adler
See Recommended Producers.

Stube
See Restaurants.

 RESTAURANTS

Schwarzer Adler
See Recommended Producers.

Stube
Winterstrasse 28
D 79346 Kiechlinsbergen
Tel: (07642) 1786
Light and classic cooking, good wine list and (a few) very pleasant rooms. Friendly prices.

 PLACES OF INTEREST

Breisach
Before the Romans erected fortifications this was a celtic strong point. There is an impressive 13th–14th-century Münster and the climb up to the old town is worth it if only for the views of the Rhine and Kaiserstuhl.

Limberg. At the peak of the Limberg stands the Burgruine Sponeck, a ruined 13th-century castle rebuilt during the 1920s – unfortunately, however, without regard for historical authenticity.

Perhaps the best wines from Sasbach are the Rieslings made by the Bercher estate of nearby Burkheim, which seems able to make exciting wines from every grape variety that will grow here. Of all the Kaiserstuhl wine towns and villages Burkheim is the richest in history: the centre looks as if nothing has changed for the last two centuries. Cars must be parked outside the impressive town gates. From here there is perhaps the best view up to the peak of the Kaiserstuhl, the Totenkopf or 'Death's Head', crowned with a radio mast that adds a slightly menacing accent to the landscape.

It is only a few minutes' drive from here to Bischoffingen and the estate of Karl Heinz Johner, Baden's great pioneer of new-oak-ageing for white and red wines. His new winery is hard to miss since it looks as if it has been beamed in from the California of the 21st century. The edifice is quite a contrast to the garages in which he made and matured his first wines during the late 1980s.

Another short drive brings you to Oberrotweil, home to another of the area's great all-rounders, Wolf-Dietrich Salwey, who makes marvellous fruit brandies in addition to fine white, rosé and red wines. Just around the corner lies the imposing residence of the Freiherr von Gleichenstein, owner of one of the area's largest estates. Sadly, the wines are not as impressive as the house, the 16th-century cellars or walled gardens.

The climb up to Oberbergen should not be missed. This is not only because of the small town's picturesque position nestling between terraced vineyards, nor even because of the Keller family's excellent wine estate, but because the Kellers also run one of the best restaurants in Baden: Schwarzer Adler. Having paused here for as long as it takes to absorb its many delights, you can take the road

over the top of the Kaiserstuhl and down through woods and vineyards to Bötzingen, the most important winegrowing community on its eastern side. Bötzingen's dynamic cooperative is particularly well known for its succulent Weissburgunder. However, if time is limited follow the road back down to Oberrotweil and from here around the base of the Kaiserstuhl to Achkarren, whose cooperative makes rich, deliberately old-fashioned wines.

Arguably the most important stop on any serious tour is Ihringen, whose towering, buttressed Winklerberg is probably the best vineyard site in the entire Kaiserstuhl. Its volcanic soil gives intensely minerally dry Weissburgunder and Grauburgunder. The leading producers of these wines are the Dr Heger and Stigler estates.

Joachim Heger also makes some very concentrated Spätburgunder reds from the Winklerberg and a fair amount of red wine from the Tuniberg (sold under his second label) only five kilometres from Ihringen. Here the best vineyards, the Kapellenberg of Münzingen, lie like those of the Kaiserstuhl at its southwestern tip.

Above and bottom left *The slopes of the Kaiserstuhl have been remodelled on a massive scale to form large terraces for vineyards.*

Burkheim
An idyllic small wine town with a magnificent gate house and many fine old houses. Look out for the ruined Schwendi-Schloss.

Endingen
The late-Gothic Rathaus and Marktbrunnen fountain, Renaissance Kornhaus, 18th-century Neues Rathaus and many fine houses from the 17th and 18th centuries lie in the streets around the Marktplatz.

FESTIVAL

Ihringen
The well known 'Weintage' wine festival in the main street takes place in early June. It would be hard to imagine a better event of this kind.

FREIBURG AND BREISGAU

RECOMMENDED PRODUCERS

Dr Heger
See Recommended Producers
(Kaiserstuhl and Tuniberg).

Bernhard Huber
Heimbacher Weg 19
D 79364 Malterdingen
Tel: (07644) 1200
One of the brightest new stars
among Baden's winemakers,
Bernhard Huber's concentrated,
sophisticated Spätburgunder
reds are first rank. His rich dry
Weissburgunder, Grauburgunder
and Chardonnay have also
improved in leaps and bounds.
Strictly by appointment only.

Salwey
See Recommended Producers
(Kaiserstuhl and Tuniberg).

Stigler
See Recommended Producers
(Kaiserstuhl and Tuniberg).

Below *Watchtowers with glazed
tiles jut from Freiburg's ancient
Kaufhaus, which is still used for
official city functions. Statues of
the Habsburg emperors (1530)
lie behind the Gothic façade.*

FREIBURG AND BREISGAU

Freiburg is one of the most beautiful cities in Baden and the natural choice as a base from which to tour the southern half of the region. It could hardly be more idyllic, sitting as it does between the Kaiserstuhl and the hills of the Breisgau where the Höllental valley enters that of the Rhine. Although it was virtually destroyed in 1944, the town has been rebuilt and restored over a period of 30 years with loving attention to detail.

Almost the only building to escape the destruction was Freiburg's famous Münster. Though not as large or imposing as the Münsters of Strassbourg or Basel it is one of the masterpieces of German Gothic architecture. Perhaps this is because its construction was spread over four centuries, beginning shortly after the town's foundation in the early years of the 12th century. In spite of the city's growth to almost 200,000 inhabitants during the last century and a half, the pinnacle of the Münster's graceful spire dominates the town as it did when it was completed in 1320.

However, it is not just the Münster and other fine old buildings in the surrounding streets that give Freiburg its special atmosphere. Rather it is the way in which the architecture continues to provide a frame for the city's vibrant life. Go to the Münsterplatz Markt on a weekday morning and you feel this most strongly. The market is always buzzing with locals and students from the university. You may even see one of the town's top chefs making last-

minute purchases. Badener's have a sanguine humour and an appreciation of the good things in life that have much in common with the French *joie de vivre*. Trades-people and professionals, shoppers and visitors mix with cosmopolitan ease. In the narrow streets of the old town (a dangerous zone for compulsive shoppers!) you are sure to find tourists but somehow they seem to be absorbed into the fabric of the town however numerous they are.

HOTELS

Colombi
See Restaurants.
Markgräfler Hof
See Restaurants.

RESTAURANTS

Hotel Colombi
Restaurant Hans-Thoma-Stube
Am Colombi-Park, D 79098 Freiburg
Tel: (0761) 21060
Director Roland Burtsche and chef Alfred Klink make this the place to dine in style. Both international cuisine (in Colombi) and regional (in the Hans-Thoma-Stube) excellent. As a hotel it meets the highest international standard with prices to match.
Eichhalde
Stadtstrasse 91
D 79104 Freiburg-Herdern
Tel: (0761) 54817
Matthias Dahlinger's small, popular restaurant in the outskirts of Freiburg offers excellent value for money.
Hotel-Restaurant
Markgräfler Hof
Gerberau 22, D 79098 Freiburg
Tel: (0761) 32540
Hans-Leo Kempchen's creative international-style cuisine is organised around the best seasonal ingredients (often local); the wine list draws enthusiasts from all over Germany and beyond. Outstanding range of Baden and Bordeaux wines. Simple but pleasant hotel rooms are as reasonably priced as the wine and food.

Above *The tower crowning the Münster's west façade is one of few church towers in the country to have been wholly completed in the Middle Ages. Only the transept crossing and its two flanking towers remain of the original Romanesque building which was begun c1200.* Left *The Münsterplatz, surrounded by buildings redolent of municipal or ecclesiastical prestige, is brought to life each weekday by the noise and bustle of a busy market.*

PLACES OF INTEREST:

Emmendingen
The 11th-century Hochburg is the largest ruined castle in southern Baden and still towers over the surrounding country.

Freiburg Museums
Augustinermuseum
Augustinerplatz
A large collection of art and artifacts from the Middle Ages.

Museum für Ur- und Frühgeschichte
Colombischlössle
Archeological museum in a magnificent mid-19th-century mansion.

Museum für Neue Kunst
Marienstrasse
A fine collection of modern art, the emphasis on Germany from the 1920s to the present day.

Glottertal
This beautiful valley that climbs into the Black Forest just north of Freiburg has a perfectly situated outdoor swimming pool.

Freiburg's many architectural high points include the magnificent Renaissance Kaufhaus on the Münsterplatz, the Altes Rathaus on the Rathausplatz and the Martinstor and Schwabentor city gates.

The Augustinermuseum's collection of paintings and sculptures from the Middle Ages and the Museum für Ur- und Frühgeschichte's display of celtic artifacts are also worth devoting time to, followed of course by a welcome and refreshing visit to one of the town's many good Weinstuben and/or restaurants.

Although the restaurant in Hotel Colombi is among Baden's very finest, the town's large student population and the locals' love of good food means that you do not have to spend a fortune to eat well here.

Freiburg may not be renowned as a wine town but in the Schlossberg it possesses one of the Breisgau's finest vineyards. Its highest point can be reached by cable car from the Stadt Garten.

The Breisgau has perhaps the lowest profile of all Baden's sub-regions because until recently the only really good wines from its vineyards were made by estates situated

elsewhere. The Rieslings and Rivaners from the Freiburger Schlossburg by the Stigler estate of Ihringen and the filigree dry Spätburgunder rosé wines from the Glottertal made by Wolf-Dietrich Salwey have long enjoyed good reputations. However, these producers are based in the Kaiserstuhl and their successes have therefore done little to promote the reputation of the Breisgau.

But this situation has changed recently and in a way that says much about the power of a single producer to influence the standing of a winegrowing area. In 1987 Bernhard Huber of Malterdingen (see map page 36, ref B6) left the local winemaking cooperative. Since then his powerful Spätburgunder red wines and new-oak-aged whites have enabled him to establish himself as one of the star producers of Baden alongside the leading estates of the Kaiserstuhl and Ortenau.

Because of the lack of independent wine producers and inactivity on the part of the cooperative here the potential of the local vineyards was virtually unknown. Now Huber has purchased land in the once-famous Schlossberg site of Hecklingen directly below the ruined castle of Burg Lichteneck. This could be the beginning of a new era for the Breisgau.

Above The peaceful village square of Auggen in Baden.
Left Early morning sun on the verdant slopes of a small farm in Glottertal.
Below The Münster's pierced octagonal belfry is surmounted by an openwork spire whose delicacy belies its medium of stone.

SCHWARZWALD

HOTELS

**Hotel and Restaurant
Bareiss/Dorfstuben/Kaminstube**
Gärtenbühlweg 14
D 72270 Baiersbonn-Mitteltal
Tel: (07442) 470
Hermann Bareiss' superb spa hotel is
very well equipped for some sport
or exercise after too many tastings
and good meals. Simplicity and clarity
of flavour, guiding principles of top
chef Claus-Peter Lumpp, find full
expression in Restaurant Bareiss. In
the Dorfstuben and Kaminstube the
country cooking is excellent.

**Schlosshotel Bühlerhöhe/
Restaurant Imperial**
Schwarzwaldhochstrasse 1
D 77652 Bühl
Tel: (07226) 55100
Max Gründig invested DM150
million in transforming this castle into
a luxury hotel. The architecture,
surrounding park and magnificent
view over the valley are as
impressive as the prices. Wolfgang
Müller's refined cooking makes the
restaurant alone worth a detour.

Spielweg
Spielweg 61
D 79244 Obermünstertal
Tel: (07636) 7090
This family-run, moderately priced
hotel is half-an-hour's drive from
Freiburg, high in the Black Forest.
Karl-Josef Fuch's regional dishes are
packed with flavour and the service
is excellent. Indoor and outdoor
swimming pools, tennis courts, etc.

**Wald- und Sporthotel
Traube/Schwarzwaldstube/
Köhlerstube/Bauernstube**
Tonbachstrasse
D 72270 Baiersbonn-Tonbach
Tel: (07442) 4920
(Restaurants) (07442) 492665
This luxury spa hotel has everything
you could ask and rooms are
relatively good value. The intensely
flavoured, precisely balanced
creations of perfectionist Harald
Wohlfahrt in the Schwarzwaldstube
restaurant are sublime. Tables for
dinner must be booked far in
advance; reservation is essential for
lunch. In the Köhlerstube the
standard is high but the cuisine
rather less grand; the Bauernstube
offers excellent regional cooking.

Right and far right *Even in
the densely forested environs
of Lake Titisee, the importance
of wholesome sustenance is
not forgotten.*

SCHWARZWALD

Many visitors come to Baden for its wine, others for its fine
cooking. (Only Vienna, with its Sachertorte and Apfel-
strudel, can match the Schwarzwald and its Kirschtorte in
having become world-famous through the popularity of a
cake.) Still more come to see for themselves the region's
great natural beauty, particularly the magnificent scenery of
the Schwarzwald, or Black Forest.

This range of densely forested mountains runs north
from where the Rhine forms the Swiss-German border to
Karlsruhe. The region looks at its best in spring when the
mountains' lower slopes are dusted with cherry blossom
and snow still clings to the peaks.

Although the Schwarzwald is a favourite tourist destination
for Germans as well as for foreign visitors, only a few of the
best known towns and villages ever seem crowded. Towns
like the well-appointed and luxurious Baden-Baden have
excluded the masses by being so fearfully expensive.

The forest's highest peaks and its most dramatic scenery
lie just to the south and east of Freiburg and are best
reached from there. Take the B31 along the Höllental to
Titisee, the almost impossibly pretty Schwarzwald town on
the bank of a small lake, surrounded by mountains. From
here it is only a short drive to the Schluchsee (take the
B500), the largest lake in the mountains; or past the peaks

of the Feldberg and Bellchen (follow the B500 to Bärental then the B317, direction Schopfheim/Basel). The views from both these peaks are spectacular. The Bellchen peak can be reached by car if you have the patience (and your car the strength of drive-shaft) to negotiate a hundred bends in the road.

The other high-point of the Schwarzwald is a gastronomic one at the spa town of Baiersbonn to the east of Offenburg. The quickest route is by leaving the A5 *Autobahn* at the Appenweier exit just north of Offenburg and driving east along the B28 through the Schwarzwald to Freundstadt, then the last seven kilometres along the B462. Allow an hour; longer if you wish to stop to admire the scenery. Views along the even more tortuous Schwarzwaldhochstrasse (B500) from Baden-Baden are yet more spectacular (allow up to two hours).

Baiersbonn is actually composed of a string of villages along the valley of the River Murg. Here you are spoiled for choice of first-class hotels and restaurants. Even in the second restaurants of Hotel Traube in Tonbach or Hotel Bareiss in Mitteltal you can expect a gastronomic experience that would put the best restaurants of many large German towns to shame. Similarly, the town's best hotels are among the finest in the country: the standard of comfort and facilities certainly justifies a detour. Needless to say, however, such perfection has its price.

Above *The lower slopes of the Black Forest protect the vineyards of the research station Schloss Ortenberg from cold easterly winds.*

RESTAURANTS

Bareiss
See Hotels.
Dorfstuben/Kaminstube
See Hotels: Bareiss.
Imperial
See Hotels: Schlosshotel.
Köhlerstube/Bauernstube
See Hotels: Traube, Baiersbonn.
Schwarzwaldstube
See Hotels: Traube.
Spielweg
See Hotels.

PLACES OF INTEREST

St Blasien
The Klosterkirche of this small town high in the Black Forest is a masterpiece of early neo-Classicism.
Lake Titisee
Formed by a moraine barrier, this pretty lake lies at the junction of several tourist routes.
Wolfach
The 17th-century Schloss of Wolfach is an impressive monument, as is the 13th-century chapel.
Zell
The 15th-century Lange Turm is the largest remaining piece of this small city-state's ancient defences. The town centre contains many 18th and some 17th-century buildings.

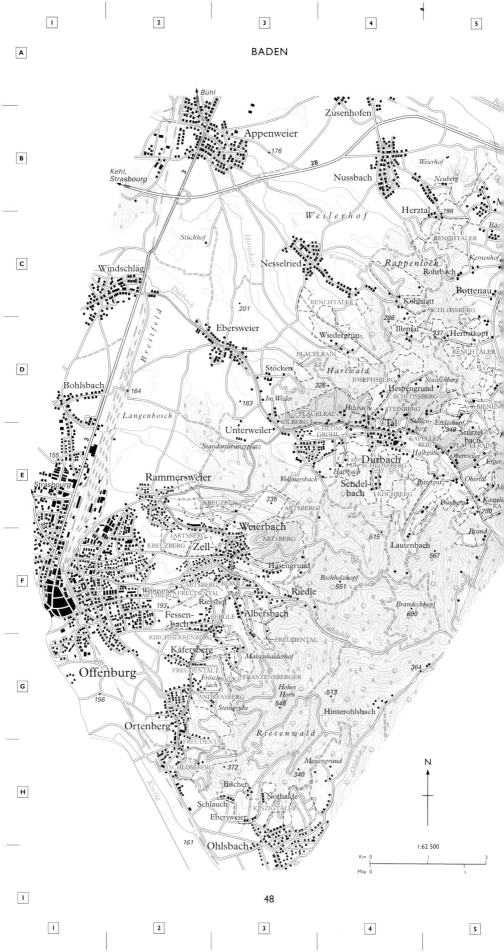

Bühl

Zusenhofen

Appenweier

176

Kehl,
Strasbourg

28

Nussbach

3

Weierhof

Neuberg

Weilerhof

Herztal

198

RENCHTALER

Bäc

Stückhof

Nesselried

Wannenbach

Rappenloch

Rohrbach

Kohlstatt

Bottenau

Kernenhof

Windschläg

Durbach

201

RENCHTALER

286

SCHLOSSBERG

Ebersweier

Wiedergrün

Illental

337

Herbstkopf

PLAUELRAIN

RENCHTALER

Stöcken

Hartwald

326

JOSEPHSBERG

Staufenberg

Bohlsbach

164

Im Weiler

183

PLAUELRAIN

Hilsbach

Hespengrund

SCHLOSSBERG

BIENE

Langenbosch

KOLBERG

SCHLOSS
GROHL

STEINBERG

Tal

Stöllen-
berg

Erleskopf

349

Stürzel-
bach

Unterweiler

Standortübungsplatz

155

3

Durbach

KAPELLEN
BERG

Halbgütle

PLAUELRAIN

Oberweiler

Erger

Strasbourg

Rammersweier

KREUZBERG

235

ABTSBERG

Hartbach

SCHLOSSBERG

Sendel-
bach

KOCHBERG

Rüttergut

Ritterg

Dinnbg

Obertd

Kassel
KA

250

Vollmersbach

Brand

Weierbach

ABTSBERG

515

Lautenbach

ABTSBERG

Zell

KREUZBERG

Hasengrund

567

Tischholzkopf
551

Brandeckkopf
690

ABTSBERG

BERGLE

Riedle

Weingarten
ABTSBERG

FREUDENTAL

193

Riesshof

Albersbach

Talbächle

Fessen-
bach

BERGLE

FREUDENTAL

KIRCHHERRENBERG

364

Käfersberg

Maisenhalderhof

Offenburg

FREUDENTAL

Frösch
lach

FRANZENSBERGER

Hohes
Horn
546

513

156

ANDREASBERG

Steingrube

Hinterohlsbach

Ortenberg

Riesenwald

FREUDENTAL

SCHLOSSBERG

372

Meisengrund

340

Bächen

N

Schlauch

Nothalde

KINZIGTALER

Ebersweier

1:62 500

161

Ohlsbach

Km 0   1   2

Mile 0   1

Kinzig

Right The tower of the 19th-century Wilhelmine Castle above Ortenberg.

Baden: Ortenau

ORTENAU

If the wines of Ortenau, which stretches from Baden–Baden to just south of Offenburg, are not particularly well known it is paradoxically because the region has such abundant natural charms and produces large quantities of good wine. Its picturesque towns and villages nestling amongst vine-clad and forested hills are popular tourist destinations. The ease with which most good producers sell to visitors and loyal private customers leaves them with little incentive to strive for optimum quality.

The vineyards on these undulating hillsides at the foot of the Black Forest have enormous potential. The mountains to the east form an effective barrier to cold winds and where there are sheltered south-facing slopes, extremely favourable micro-climates exist. During warm summer evenings cool air flows down into the vineyards from the forests above, creating dramatic differences between day- and night-time temperatures. This together with the weathered granite soils gives the wines their elegance and aromatic delicacy. Riesling (also called Klingelberger here), Gewürztraminer and Scheurebe all flourish. They give wines with a similar amount of body to those from the Middle Haardt area of the Pfalz, but with a more restrained bouquet. Even Gewürztraminer (often called Clevner here),

Above *Harvest time at the Schloss Staufenberg estate.*

ORTENAU

RECOMMENDED PRODUCERS

Winzergenossenschaft Durbach
Nachweide 2, D 77770 Durbach
Tel: (0781) 93660
Geppert and cellarmaster Wörner produce good dry and naturally sweet Riesling and Gewürztraminer as well as substantial Spätburgunder reds and pleasant Müller-Thurgau at this top co-op. Closed Saturday and Sunday afternoons.

Freiherr Franckenstein
Weingartenstrasse 66
D 77654 Offenburg
Tel: (0781) 34973
One of the most reliable producers in the Ortenau producing rich, substantial dry Rieslings, Grauburgunder and Gewürztraminer. Appointment essential at weekends.

Graf Wolff Metternich
Grohl 26, D 77770 Durbach
Tel: (0781) 42779
Ottmar Schilli has directed this large estate for many years, maintaining a high standard across the large range. Excellent dry Riesling and magnificent Riesling and Scheurebe dessert wines. Appointment

a wine which can easily be bloated, cloying and bitter, yields sleek, refined wines. The vivid fruit of the white wines is matched by that of the Spätburgunder reds which are perhaps the most charming and immediately appealing red wines made in all Germany. The grape's close relatives Weissburgunder and Grauburgunder are also widely cultivated in Ortenau and give pleasant mid-weight wines but they rarely gain either the richness of the best examples from the Kaiserstuhl or the racy elegance of those from the Kraichgau to the north. Whether this has more to do with winemakers' priorities and ambitions than with the climate or soil is not clear.

The heart of Ortenau lies just to the east of Offenburg and here, particularly around Durbach, the greatest concentration of top vineyards is found. To reach the area take the B3 north (direction Bühl/Baden-Baden), turning off to the right towards Ebersweier. For the last few kilometres follow signs to Durbach.

Vineyards cover the Durbach Valley which cuts into the foothills of the Black Forest. The river's east-west course creates a huge area of south-facing vineyards and one of Baden's most beautiful vineyard landscapes. The charming town with its well kept houses and fine hotels is strung out beneath the vineyards. Bus groups seldom come here, only wine tourists.

Just over two thirds of Durbach's 470 hectares of vineyard belong to members of its extremely well run co-operative: unquestionably one of the best in Baden and indeed in Germany as a whole. Unusually for Baden many of its leading estates bear aristocratic names and their headquarters are in imposing residences – none more so than Schloss Staufenberg, which stands on a ridge high above the vineyards (ask directions in the town). The view from the castle terrace in fine weather is as breathtaking as anything the Mosel or Rhine valleys have to offer. Baden's first Riesling vines were planted on the steep slopes below this Schloss in 1776.

Having descended to the main road follow the sign posts for Offenburg through verdant woodland. At Rammersweier turn off for Zell-Weierbach, one of Offenburg's winemaking suburbs. It is home to the Freiherr von und zu Franckenstein estate (Mary Shelly borrowed the name for the protagonist of her famous novel). The vineyards are not quite as steep as those in Durbach but the wines can almost match those of their more famous neighbours. This is primarily white-wine country but in the nearby village of Fessenbach there is a strong tradition for Spätburgunder red wines which the cooperative has developed successfully during recent years.

Continue through Käfersberg to Ortenberg, whose wine research station is housed in the 19th-century neo-Gothic Schloss Ortenberg. The ruined Burg nearby is far older, dating back at least to the 12th century, but like so many military installations it was destroyed by Louis XIV's troops just over three centuries ago. The ruin occupies a commanding position over the valley of the Kinzig and the Rhine itself.

The most serious competition for Durbach and environs within Ortenau comes from the Rieslings which grow in the short stretch of vineyards between Bühl and

recommended; closed Saturday afternoons and Sundays.

Andreas Laible
Am Bühl 6, D 77770 Durbach
Tel: (0781) 41238
The family's small estate is known for elegant dry Rieslings but Scheurebe, Traminer and Muskateller with natural sweetness are even better. Appointment essential Sundays.

Heinrich Männle
Sendelbach 16, D 77770 Durbach
Tel: (0781) 41101
Männle's Riesling, Scheurebe and Gewürztraminer with natural sweetness are at least as interesting as his Spätburgunder reds. Appointment essential Sundays.

Winzergenossenschaft Sasbachwalden
Talstrasse 2, D 77887 Sasbachwalden
Tel: (07841) 20290
Whites drab but Spätburgunder reds have fruit and body. Closed Sunday mornings and weekend afternoons November to April.

Schloss Neuweier
Mauerbergstrasse 21
D 76534 Neuweier
Tel: (07223) 96770
Gisela Joos and winemaker Spinner have re-established this once-famous estate. Superb dry Rieslings with a strong minerally character. Appointment essential at weekends.

Below *The town's Kochberg vineyard forms part of an orderly patchwork of vines covering 470 hectares of Durbach countryside.*

Schloss Ortenberg
Burgweg 19a
D 77799 Ortenberg
Tel: (0781) 34848
Since Winfried Köninger took over
at this research station in the
early 1990s quality has improved
dramatically. Intensely minerally dry
Rieslings and lush dessert wines are
the highlights. Appointment essential
at weekends.
Schloss Staufenberg/
Markgraf von Baden
D 77770 Durbach
Tel: (0781) 42778
Its best dry and naturally sweet
Rieslings and Spätburgunder rosé are
excellent but other wines are erratic
in quality. There are magnificent
views and an original wine restaurant
is open from March to November,
10am–8pm.

HOTELS

Brenner's Park Hotel
Schillerstrasse 6
D 76530 Baden-Baden
Tel: (07221) 9000
One of Europe's great hotels in a
beautiful park on the bank of the
Osbach in the heart of Baden-Baden.
The ultimate in luxury, comfort and
service: with prices to match!
Romatik Hotel
der Kleiner Prinz
Lichtenthaler Strasse 36
D 76530 Baden-Baden
Tel: (07221) 3464
A most attractive hotel seemingly like
a little dream world. Fair prices.

Baden-Baden to the north. Between Offenburg and Bühl
lies a stretch of idyllic wine country where vineyards
alternate with forest, orchards and gardens and each village
seems more charming than the last. To appreciate it at its
best, follow the signposted Badische Weinstrasse from
Kappelrodeck or Sasbachwalden north to Baden-Baden.
The co-operatives of both these villages consistently make
good medium-bodied Spätburgunder red wines with bright
cherry fruit and soft tannins.

Top *Magnificent stepped gables
and heavily buttressed walls add
to the commanding presence of
Schloss Ortenberg.*

Above *The Pump Room
(Trinkhalle) in the spa Park is one
of the focuses of Baden-Baden's
luxurious health resort.*

Left *Murals along the Pump Room illustrate colourful legends of the Baden countryside.*

**Hotel Talmühle/
Restaurant Le Jardin**
Talstrasse 36
D 77887 Sasbachwalden
Tel: (07841) 1001
Charming family-run hotel in a
beautiful garden. Excellent regional
cooking, modest prices.
Hotel-Restaurant Zum Ritter
Badische Weinstrasse 1
D 77770 Durbach
Tel: (0781) 31031
Attractive and comfortable hotel in a
lovingly restored 15th-century house.
Good classic cooking.

RESTAURANTS

Le Jardin
See Hotels: Talmühle.
Raub's Restaurant
Haupstrasse 41
D 76456 Kuppenheim-Oberndorf
Tel: (07225) 75623
From its Art Deco interior design
to the imaginative modern cuisine
this is not what you would expect
in deepest Baden. An excellent list of
regional wines plus a fine selection
from around the world.
Schloss Staufenberg
See Recommended Producers.
Wehlauer's Badischer Hof
Hauptstrasse 36, D 77815 Bühl
Tel: (07223) 23063
Top chef Peter Wehlauer serves
imaginative modern cooking but
quality can be erratic.

PLACES OF INTEREST

Baden-Baden
The best view of the town is from
the tower of the massive ruined
Schloss Hohenbaden. The Neues
Schloss dates from the 14th century
but most of what is seen today from
the late-16th. The excavated remains
of the Roman baths are fascinating.
Forbach (Murgtal)
Small town just above Baden-Baden:
worth the detour for the scenery
and an18th-century wooden bridge.
Gengenbach
Massive gate houses, a 12th-century
abbey church, a 15th-century
Martinskirche and a neo-Classical
Rathaus from 1784 are among many
well preserved monuments.
Rastatt
Ludwig Wilhelm Markgraf von Baden
moved his court here in the early
18th century. The massive baroque
Schloss at the town's centre is
second only to that of Mannheim.

The northern tip of Ortenau sells its wines in Bocksbeutel bottles like those of Franken. This confusing packaging should not however obscure the fact that the vineyards of Neuweier and its neighbouring villages yield some of the best dry Rieslings in Baden.

The terraced vineyards give the landscape quite a different appearance from that further south, although the granite soils are similar to those of Durbach. The newly reactivated Schloss Neuweier estate is well worth a visit.

Baden-Baden, situated in the idyllic Oosbach Valley, has been a spa town since Roman times. During the 19th century, the period from which most of its imposing buildings date, the town became one of the most highly favoured destinations for Europe's wealthy and privileged. It remains one of the wealthiest towns in Germany and is home to some of the nation's finest hotels, most notably Brenner's Park Hotel. The ruined medieval Hohenbaden castle and the 15th-century Stiftskirche are among the few buildings that date from before the destruction of the 17th century.

KRAICHGAU, BADISCHE BERGSTRASSE AND TAUBERFRANKEN

RECOMMENDED PRODUCERS

Winzergenossenschaft Beckstein
Weinstrasse 30
D 97922 Lauda-Königshofen
Tel: (09343) 5000
This co-op's high standards make
even the dry Müller-Thurgaus
fresh and fruity. Powerful dry
Weissburgunders are a speciality.
Open throughout the week.

Albert Heitlinger
Am Mülberg
D 76684 Östringen-Tiefenbach
Tel: (07259) 1061
Ignore the rustic white wines – the
Spätburgunder and Lemberger reds
are what make this medium-sized
estate interesting. Appointment
essential Sundays.

Reichsgraf und Marquis zu Hoensbroech
D 74918 Angelbachtal-Michelfeld
Tel: (07265) 381
Rudiger Graf Hoensbroech
makes supremely elegant dry
Weissburgunder. His dry Rieslings
from the Eichelberger Kapellenberg
are often good too. Visits by
appointment only.

Seeger
Rhorbacher Strasse 101
D 69181 Leimen
Tel: (06224) 72178
Winemaker Thomas Seeger's rich,
well structured Spätburgunders have
gained him a promising reputation.
New-oak-aged dry Weissburgunder
and Grauburgunder are also
impressive. The Seeger's stylish
Jägerlust wine bar is open Tuesdays
to Fridays, 6–11pm.

HOTELS

Mondial/Restaurant Chandelle
Schwetzinger Strasse 123
D 69198 Wiesloch
Tel: (06222) 5760
Unattractively modern from
the outside this small hotel is
comfortable, well run and ideally
located for touring northern Baden.
Karlheinz Schumair's creative
international cooking is of the
highest standard. Moderate prices
for this quality.

KRAICHGAU, BADISCHE BERGSTRASSE AND TAUBERFRANKEN

In the northern parts of Baden there are few large estates
or particularly active cooperatives. As a result, and perhaps
also because the scenery is less spectacular than it is further
south, the area is unjustly ignored.

The Kraichgau vineyards are scattered about the hill
country between Karlsruhe, Pforzheim, Sinsheim and
Wiesloch. The loess-loam soils which predominate are well
suited to the Pinot family; particularly Weissburgunder,
which here gives wines combining substance with a racy
elegance seldom seen in the variety. Islands of marl provide
some good sites for Riesling.

*Above right The vineyards of the
Kraichgau are generally planted on
gentle slopes.*

54

The area's best dry whites all need some time in the bottle to show of their best and are capable of gaining from five or more years' ageing. Red wine also plays a significant role, both Spätburgunder and Lemberger (the latter more familiar in Württemberg) giving some good results. The leading estate here is that of Weissburgunder specialist Reichsgraf und Marquis zu Hoensbroech in Angelbachtal-Michelfeld (follow the signs for Mülhausen, then Angelbachtal from Wiesloch).

From Wiesloch northward runs the narrow strip of vineyards which forms the Badische Bergstrasse. It lies on the last slope of the Odenwald's foothills facing west across the Rhine Rift Valley, much like the vines of neighbouring Hessische Bergstrasse to the north. Here it is rather warmer than in the Kraichgau and spring comes earlier. Although white-wine grapes dominate, the friendly climate is no less suitable for red-wine production and in recent years the Seeger estate of Leimen, just south of Heidelberg, has begun to realise this potential. The Seeger's stylish wine bar makes this estate especially worthy of a visit.

Over 100 kilometres separate the 600 hectares of vineyards in the Tauber Valley, which belong to Baden, from the main body of the region. The drive from Heidelberg up the narrow, twisting Neckar Valley (B37 to Mosbach, then across open country on the B27) is worth taking for the scenery alone, although Tauberfranken is best combined with a tour of Franken itself. The area is home to one of Baden's best winemaking cooperatives, that of Beckstein close to Lauda-Königshofen. As in the northern tip of Ortenau, most wines here are sold in the dumpy Bocksbeutel, a shape familiar in neighbouring Franken.

Parkhotel/Restaurant Gala
Deimlingstrasse 36
D 75175 Pforzheim
Tel: (07231) 1610
Imposing and comfortable hotel in the centre of Pforzheim. French-German cooking of some sophistication. Moderate prices.
Zum Ochsen
See Restaurants.

RESTAURANTS

Chandelle
See Hotels: Mondial.
Freihof
Freihofstrasse 2, D 69168 Wiesloch
Tel: (0622) 2517
In one of Wiesloch's oldest houses Bernhard Zepf runs this excellent wine restaurant. Ambitious regional cooking, an excellent list of Baden wines and friendly service. Modest prices for the quality.
Gala
See Hotels: Parkhotel.
Oberländer Weinstube
Akadamiestrasse 7
D 76133 Karlsruhe
Tel: (0721) 25066
A carefully preserved 19th-century interior, beautiful courtyard and a marvellous selection of Baden wines including rare old vintages. Chef Günter Buchmann's sophisticated cooking would also impress in much grander surroundings. Fair prices. Reservation for courtyard tables essential in fine weather!
Zum Ochsen
Pfinzstrasse 64
D 76227 Karlsruhe-Durlach
Tel: (0721) 943860
In this lovingly restored inn in a suburb of Karlsruhe Gérard Jollit serves classic French cooking as a only a Frenchman can. Excellent international wine list and a few pleasant rooms. Fair prices.

PLACES OF INTEREST

Karlsruhe
Much of Karlsruhe's classical grandeur was lost during the Second World War but the core has been lovingly restored. The Schloss, built shortly after the town's foundation in 1715, is the centrepiece. Neo-Classical architect Friedrich Weinbrenner made his mark on the town, which is home to Germany's supreme court.

Left *The late-Gothic Church of the Holy Spirit or Heilig-Geist-Kirch towers over Heidelberg and the Neckar.*

HEIDELBERG

 HOTELS

Der Europäische Hof
Friedrich-Ebert-Anlage 1
D 69117 Heidelberg
Tel: (06221) 5150
A grand hotel on the outskirts of
Heidelberg and one of Northern
Baden's best, but comfort and service
of this standard have their price!

Hirschgasse
Hirschgasse 3, D 69120 Heidelberg
Tel: (06221) 4540
Highly recommended, stylish, small
hotel. This comfortable and
beautifully preserved inn dating from
1472 is on the right bank of the
Neckar below the Philosophenweg.
Expensive.

Zum Ritter St Georg
Hauptstrasse 178
D 69117 Heidelberg
Tel: (06221) 24272
Comfortable hotel housed in an
imposing Renaissance house dating
from 1592. Moderate prices.

*Below The original Heidelberg
was laid waste and the castle on
the hillside above sacked in Louis
XIV's brutal campaign of 1689.*

HEIDELBERG

The city of Heidelberg and its partially ruined castle owe their fame to the work of a series of romantic painters. In the English-speaking world, Turner's numerous portrayals of this scene are best known. In Germany the works of Carl Philipp Fohr, Karl Rottmann and Ernst Fries, all of whom were greatly inspired by their travels in Italy, have etched themselves into the popular conscience. During the first half of the 19th century, Heidelberg became a place of cultural pilgrimage and remains such to this day. Each summer (late July to late August) a series of evening concerts and theatrical performances are staged within the courtyard of the Schloss.

The appeal of the old town, which nestles in the Neckar Valley where it opens out into the Rhine plain, is also undiminished.

Three centuries ago, just after the attacks of the French army in 1689 and 1693, Heidelberg presented a very different vista, having been reduced to rubble and ruins. One of the few buildings to escape the destruction was the magnificent Friedrichsbau within the courtyard of the Schloss. Much of the extensive castle complex remains a series of ruins whose distinctive silhouette, perched on the steep side of the Königstuhl, has become the town's hallmark.

The castle's cavernous cellar contains another of the town's landmarks, the 220,000-litre wine barrel constructed on the order of Prince Bishop Karl Theodor in 1751 for

storing taxes paid in liquid form. One shudders to imagine what this precursor of today's cheap generic wines must have tasted like.

Arguably the best view of the Schloss is from the Philosophenweg on the opposite bank of the Neckar. This is easily reached from the old town by the imposing stone Alte Brücke, built by Karl Theodor in 1786–88 as much to document his power and greatness as for practical purposes. The terraced gardens through which the Philosophenweg winds are best appreciated in the early months of the year since in this extremely sheltered position spring arrives up to three weeks earlier than it does up in the Odenwald. From here there is a steep climb up the narrow, cobbled Schlangenweg (the name has more to do with its winding course than the presence of snakes) to the Philosophenweg.

The old town of Heidelberg lies directly below the Schloss. Only one building apart from the Schloss survives from before the disaster of 1693: the hotel 'zum Ritter' (Hauptstrasse 178).

The streets owe much of their character to students of the town's university past and present: several student 'watering holes' remain much as they were at the turn of the century. At the other end of the cultural scale there are numerous museums, of which the Kurpfälzisches Museum is the most important.

Above *Medieval gates, silhouettes echoed by that of the Heilig-Geist-Kirche behind, stand guard on the Alte Brücke.*

RESTAURANTS

Simplicissimus
Ingrimstrasse 16
D 69117 Heidelberg
Tel: (06221) 183336
The sophisticated cooking in this 'bistro' is the closest you will get to good value in Heidelberg. Good international wine list with fair prices.

Zur Herrenmühle
Hauptstrasse 237/9
D 69117 Heidelberg
Tel: (06221) 12909
Good food is expensive here. Perhaps not among the region's gastronomic elite, but Günter Ueberle's modern cuisine is consistently good. Good wine list. Fairly expensive.

PLACES TO VISIT

Schwetzingen
There may be larger and grander baroque castles, but Schwetzingen's, with its magnificent gardens, is arguably the most beautiful.

Hessische Bergstrasse

Vines have stood on the last west-facing slopes of the Odenwald forest's foothills for untold centuries but the winegrowing region of Hessische Bergstrasse has existed as such only since 1971. Before that year, 470 hectares of ideally situated vineyards with magnificent views over the upper part of the Rhine Rift Valley formed a single region, the Bergstrasse, together with the vineyards immediately to the south around Heidelberg. Political factors lead to the separation of the two and forced the creation of the 'new' winegrowing region of Hessische Bergstrasse.

This is one of the few regions that benefited from the Wine Law introduced in 1971, though initially that did not seem to be the case. The region's abundant natural beauty, lovely old towns and mild climate have made it an extremely popular day-trip and weekend destination for the inhabitants of the Main-Rhine conurbation and those of nearby Ludwigshafen-Mannheim. Its small size and moderate yields mean that rather little wine ever leaves the region except in the boots of visitors' cars. Only two of the region's producers, the Domäne Bensheim (previously Staatsweingut Bergstrasse) and the Bergsträsser Winzer cooperative, are sufficiently large that their wines are known in other parts of Germany. Together they account for almost three-quarters of the region's production but very little of this has yet to find its way onto the export market.

It is both surprising and disappointing that more people do not know about the Hessische Bergstrasse, not only because it is one of the most beautiful vineyard landscapes in Germany but also because its top vineyards can give remarkable wines. The protection afforded by the forested Odenwald mountains to the east and the northern tip of the Haardt to the west allows spring to arrive earlier here than anywhere in the country. This contributes to a very long growing season which at the same time rarely suffers

Left *Drama gives way to a
quieter charm in the landscape
of this tiny region.*

Top *The 16th-century town
hall overlooks the Marktplatz of
Heppenheim an der Bergstrasse.*

from excessive heat: ideal conditions for cultivating Riesling. Not surprisingly this grape accounts for 56 per cent of vineyard plantings here and dominates hillside sites where there are stony soils. The resulting wines have most in common with those of the Nierstein-Oppenheim area of Rheinhessen and parts of the Rheingau. Where the soil is deeper and richer both Weissburgunder and Grauburgunder flourish, giving wines resembling those from the other side of the border in Baden. The workhorse grape Müller-Thurgau is grown only in the coolest locations, particularly the island of vineyards around Gross Umstadt, half-way between the main body of the region and Asschaffenburg in Franken. Its wines are simple but when well made, fresh and fruity.

When spring arrives, hillsides become a sea of almond, peach, apricot and cherry blossom and visitors start to pour into the region. Tourists looking for cheap souvenirs might be disappointed at the region's lack of kitsch: most visitors are attracted by the number of winegrowers who have small wine bars (*Gutsauschank* or the simpler *Strauswirtschaft*), several of which are amongst the best wine restaurants in Germany. On a fine summer evening it can be difficult to find a table here, such is the appeal of this idyllic region and its charming wines.

The Hessische Bergstrasse is most easily reached by the A5 *Autobahn*. From either north or south take the Weinheim exit, turn onto the B3 northward, direction Heppenheim. This town stands at the foot of vine-clad hills and is crowned by the ruined Starkenburg castle. Half-timbered houses cluster around the old marketplace where

Below *The slopes of the Zwingenburg's Steingeröll vineyard are well suited to Riesling.*

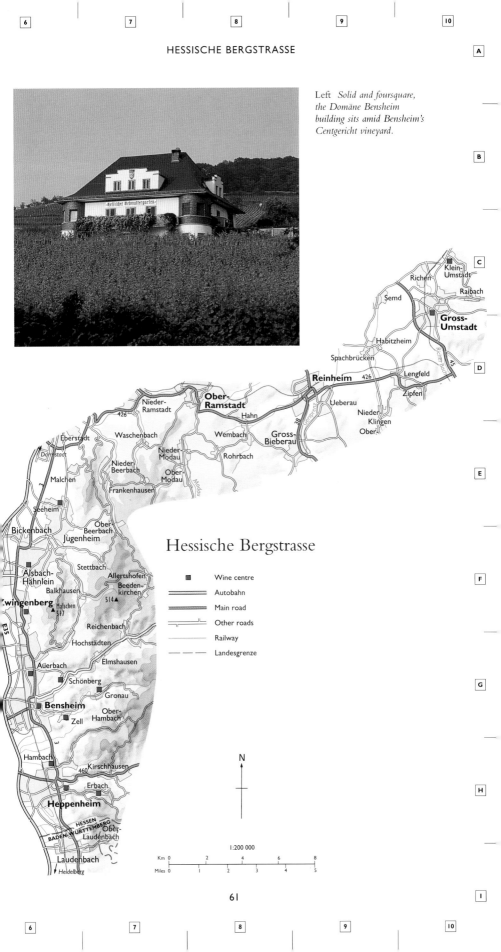

Left *Solid and foursquare,
the Domäne Bensheim
building sits amid Bensheim's
Centgericht vineyard.*

Hessische Bergstrasse

Klein-Umstadt
Richen
Raibach
Semd
Gross-Umstadt
Habitzheim
Spachbrücken
Reinheim 426
Lengfeld
Zipfen
Ober-Ramstadt
Nieder-Ramstadt
Hahn
Ueberau
Nieder-Klingen
426
Waschenbach
Wembach
Gross-Bieberau
Ober.
Eberstadt
Darmstadt
Nieder-Modau
Rohrbach
Nieder-Beerbach
Ober-Modau
Malchen
Frankenhausen
Modau
Seeheim
Ober-Beerbach
Bickenbach
Jugenheim
Stettbach
Allertshofen
Alsbach-Hähnlein
Beeden-kirchen
Balkhausen
514▲
Zwingenberg
Malschen ▲517
Reichenbach
Hochstädten
E35
Elmshausen
Auerbach
Schönberg
Gronau
Bensheim
Ober-Hambach
Zell
Hambach
Kirschhausen
460
Erbach
Heppenheim
HESSEN
BADEN-WÜRTTEMBERG
Ober-Laudenbach
Laudenbach
Heidelberg

	Wine centre
	Autobahn
	Main road
	Other roads
	Railway
	Landesgrenze

N

1:200 000

Km 0   2   4   6   8
Miles 0   1   2   3   4   5

Right *The Odenwald forest rises behind the vineyards of Zell near Bensheim.*
Far right *A lush green vinescape at Heppenheim.*

HESSISCHE BERGSTRASSE

RECOMMENDED PRODUCERS

Domäne Bensheim
Grieselstrasse 34–36
D 64625 Bensheim
Tel: (06251) 3107
Heinrich Hillenbrand is the third generation of his family to direct this estate and with cellarmaster Volker Hörr maintains high standards. Dry Weissburgunder and Grauburgunder from the Heppenheimer Centgericht site and dry Rieslings from the Heppenheimer Steinkopf and Bensheimer Kalkgasse are the region's best. Also excellent BA, TBA and Eiswein. Appointment essential at weekends.

Bergsträsser Winzer
Darmstädter Strasse 56
D 64646 Heppenheim
Tel: (06252) 73015
With new director Otto Guthier the already solid standard of this co-op's wines is rising. Look for Auslese, BA and TBA dessert wines which are often excellent value. Closed Saturday afternoons and Sundays.

Simon-Bürkle
Wiesenpromenade 13
D 64673 Zwingenberg
Tel: (06251) 76446
Kurt Simon and Wilfried Bürkle met at the Weinsberg wine school and founded this very promising estate only five years ago. Riesling, Grauburgunder and Weissburgunder dominate. *Gutsauschank* (wine bar) open from 5pm Monday–Friday, from 11am at weekends. For tastings, appointment essential at weekends.

H Freiberger
Hermannstrasse 16
D 64646 Heppenheim
Tel: (06252) 2457
Father and son Heinz Snr and Jnr concentrate on dry Riesling. Quality is mixed but there are some good wines. Appointment recommended. Closed Wednesday and Saturday afternoons and Sundays.

Weingut der Stadt Bensheim
Darmstädter Strasse 6
D 64625 Bensheim
Tel: (06251) 14269
Cellarmaster Ellen Ittner makes substantial dry Rieslings which in good vintages can be amongst the region's best wines. Appointment essential at weekends.

streets and alleys converge. The houses date from around 1700 though parts of the Rathaus or town hall are a century and a half older. The nearby stone-built Hee'schen Hof (today a school) also dates from the last years of the 17th century and there is a wealth of fine old houses to be found in the streets of the old town.

From the suburb of Hambach rise the steep terraces of the Heppenheimer Steinkopf, the region's one indisputably great vineyard. Its history goes back to 1517 and its weathered sandstone soil gives Riesling wines with considerable elegance and a pronounced minerally character.

Bensheim, just five kilometres to the north, is the centre of the region in more than one sense. Like Heppenheim its hub is the Marktplatz, which still hosts an active fruit and vegetable market every weekday. The heart of Bensheim also boasts many fine half-timbered houses from the last years of the 17th and early-18th centuries and the large pedestrian-only area in the centre of town makes it easier to admire its monuments on foot. Some remnants of the town wall can be seen in courtyards of the Obergasse, at the end of which stands the Roter Turm tower erected around 1300. The imposing Walderdorffer Hof in the same street is a marvellous example of late-Gothic half-timbered construction dating from 1470. The Haus Bensheim in the Hauptstrasse was built as an inn in 1597.

Bensheim's finest vineyards are the Kalkgasse and Streichling; the town is also home to Domäne Bensheim, a short walk from the town centre and far and away the region's leading quality wine producer. Founded in 1904 it is now one of the finest of Germany's State domaines.

The Auerbacher Schloss just north of Bensheim is a massive set of ruined fortifications dating from the 14th and 15th centuries. After Louis XIV's troops sacked it in 1674, only the hard climb involved in its approach prevented its stone from being plundered for building use by the local population. Since the early 19th century it has had a magnetic appeal for visitors to the region who continue to climb the 350 metres to admire the ruins and the splendid view over the Rhine plain. In July and August a series of theatrical performances are staged here [Tel: (06251) 2332 for information and tickets]. Above Auerbach lies the additional attraction of the Fürstenlager park, whose construction and landscaping began in the second half of the 18th century. This extravagant amusement park for the local aristocracy was laid out around the spring discovered there at the beginning of the century. The imposing Herrenhaus, now a hotel, restaurant and café, was completed in 1792.

The next town to the north is Zwingenberg. Part of its town wall is still intact and easily visible from the B3. The so-called Schlösschen, constructed at the beginning of the

Tobias Georg Seitz
Weidgasse 8
D 64625 Bensheim-Auerbach
Tel: (06251) 75825
Dry Rieslings dominate production at the Schott family's small estate. Appointment essential at weekends.

RESTAURANTS

Alchemia
Grosser Markt 5, D 64646 Heppenheim
Tel: (06252) 2326
Good-quality modern cooking and a wide selection of local wines in an 18th-century half-timbered house.

Da Gianni
R 7, 34, D 68161 Mannheim
Tel: (0621) 20326
Definitely worth the 35-km drive to what is probably Germany's top Italian restaurant. Sophisticated food and surroundings, excellent wine list – prices correspondingly high.

Dalberger Hof
Dalberger Gasse 15
D 64625 Bensheim
Tel: (06251) 4747
Restaurant with good regional cooking housed in the 'Bürgerhaus' of Bensheim. Moderate prices.

Gasthaus und Weinstube Ratsstübchen
Obergasse 1, D 64673 Zwingenberg
Tel: (06251) 72182
Authentic wine bar with wine from the owner's vineyards and meat from his own slaughterhouse.

Schlinkenkeller
Schlinkengasse 7
D 64625 Bensheim
Tel: (06251) 62323
Cellar *Weinstube* with hearty local cooking and a good selection of local wines.

Weinhaus Blauer Aff
Kappengasse 2, D 64625 Bensheim
Tel: (06251) 72958
Peter Poth's wine restaurant in picturesque Auerbach is a Bergstrasse institution. The food is simple but the range of local, French and Italian wines superb. Prices friendly. Reservation essential at weekends.

Weinschänke Rebenhof
Gartenfeld 26
D 64673 Zwingenberg
Tel: (06251) 72182
Rustic wine bar with traditional local cooking and wine from the estate's own vineyards.

Winzerkeller
Amstgasse 5, D 64646 Heppenheim
Tel: (06252) 5228
Cosy *Weinstube* with good local cooking. The wines are limited to those from the local cooperative.

HOTELS

Hotel am Bruchsee
Am Bruchsee 1
D 64646 Heppenheim
Tel: (06252) 9600
Heppenheim's best hotel. Fair prices.

Hotel Goldener Engel
Grosser Markt 2
D 64646 Heppenheim
Tel: (06252) 2563
Small, reasonably comfortable hotel in a half-timbered house right in the centre of old Heppenheim.

Parkhotel Herrenhaus
Im Staatspark Fürstenlager
D 64625 Bensheim-Auerbach
Tel: (06251) 72274
Comfortable small hotel in the Fürstenlager park 3km north of Bensheim. Moderate prices.

Right The 12th-century Klosterkirche in Lorsch was used by the townspeople until the beginning of the century for drying their tobacco. The industry is documented in the town's Tabakmuseum.

16th century, includes one of the fortifying towers from the town wall. Once again around the Marktplatz there are a number of magnificent old buildings including the Freihof of 1603 and the Hoferite of 1607. Just around the corner in the Obertor stands the magnificent Jagdschloss, which was built around 1561–3.

Behind the town rises the 517-metre peak of the Malschen and there are magnificent views from the Melibokus viewing point close to the summit. On the northwestern slope stands the ruined Alsbacher Schloss which has been partially reconstructed and restored. The Steingeröll vineyard gives the town's finest wines – the best of these being the Rieslings, which have a similar elegance to those from Bensheim.

Though Seeheim just to the north has few vines its suburb Jugenheim has some magnificent buildings. The oldest is the Bergkirche church of 1263. The Gartensaal of the late-neo-Classical Schloss Heiligenberg (1863–77) is used for art exhibitions. A short drive further brings you to Darmstadt with its many museums and the artists' colony of Mathildenhöhe.

At the northern tip of the Hessische Bergstrasse, half-way between the cities of Frankfurt and Mannheim, lies the town of Darmstadt which in spite of its modest size contains a large number of museums and a wealth of remarkable architecture. The patronage of the Grand Dukes of Hessen-Darmstadt during the 19th and early-20th centuries is primarily responsible for these riches. The Schloss at the town's centre is one of the few important buildings that predate this period. The oldest parts of the building, which has been enlarged and restyled several times during its long history, date from the late

Middle Ages. The neo-Classical St Ludwigskirche on the Wilhelminenplatz with its huge dome is in complete contrast to this eclecticism. It was designed by the architect Georg Müller who was a leading force in shaping the expanding town during the early decades of the 19th century. Sadly much of his other work in Darmstadt was destroyed during the latter part of the Second World War.

The second period of aesthetic development in Darmstadt just under a century later has thankfully left more lasting traces. These are to be found on the Mathildenhöhe just to the east of the town centre which was one of the centres of Art Nouveau in Germany, although the Mathildenhöhe's most prominent buildings hardly fit into this picture. The Russian chapel was constructed on the orders of the Russian Tsar Nikolaus II whose wife Alice was a sister of Ernst Ludwig Grand Duke of Hessen. The extraordinary Art Nouveau-Expressionist Hochszeitsturm tower with its five-fingered roof was designed by Josef Maria Olbrich and constructed by Darmstadt to celebrate Ernst Ludwig's own marriage. Olbrich was one of Germany's leading Art Nouveau architects and a collection of his finest buildings stand on the Mathildenhöhe: the Ernst-Ludwig-Haus (now home to the museum documenting the Mathildenhöhe's history) the Grosse and Kleine Glükkerthaus and the Haus Deiters which now houses the town's museum of 19th-century paintings). Another museum on the Mathildenhöhe, the Braun Design Collection, documents the development of industrial design during the last 40 years in complete contrast to the extravagances of Art Nouveau.

Above *Cheek-by-jowl, old and new buildings blend harmoniously in the small town of Zwingenberg.*

PLACES OF INTEREST

Lorsch
Lovely old town near Bensheim (between the A5 and A67) with a magnificent early-18th-century half-timbered Rathaus.

Darmstadt Museums
Hessische Landesmuseum
Friedensplatz 1
Collections of paintings from Gothic to modern periods, Art Nouveau and more. Closed Mondays.

Grossherzogliche Porzellansammlung
Prinz Georg Palais
Schlossgartenstrasse 7
18th- and 19th-century porcelain.

Schlossmuseum
Im Schloss
Collections of clothes, furniture and paintings previously owned by the Dukes of Hessen.

Museum Künsterkolonie Darmstadt
Alexandraweg 26, Mathildenhöhe
Documents the artists' colony at the turn of the century.

Württemberg

The undulating country surrounding the Neckar and its tributaries forms a unique winegrowing region. Württemberg, dotted with old towns that have survived the ravages of countless wars, stands out not only because of the special characteristics of the vineyards but also because of the distinctive human landscape. This is the one region in Germany where wine is as important a part of the inhabitants' daily diet as it is in France or Italy. The Swabians' attachment to their daily 'Viertele' (quarter litre) of wine is as important a factor in the character of Württemberg's wines as the warm dry summers of its continental climate. The Viertele is generally of a pale red wine from either the Trollinger (known as Vernatsch in Italy) or the Schwarzriesling (Pinot Meunier) grape.

Red wine has always been important here. During the the late-16th century red grapes dominated in the region's 45,000 hectares of vineyard. In those days the red and white grapes were harvested together – hence the Swabians' taste for pale red wines. 'Schillerwein' is the contemporary name for wines made from red and white grapes, the name referring to the wine's colour rather than the poet and playwright.

Whilst white grapes came to dominate in almost every other German winegrowing region during the 19th century, Württemberg's growers remained true to their red-wine traditions. Today the region's 11,200 hectares produce fully 40 per cent of all Germany's red wine.

The continental climate and the protection offered by the Odenwald to the north and the Schwäbische Alb to the south combine to produce warm, dry summers that are ideally suited to ripening red grapes. Add to these the heavy marl and gypsum marl soils typical of the region and a south-facing hillside and you have excellent conditions for producing high-quality red wines.

Left Old houses crowd along the Neckar's peaceful riverfront at Tübingen.

Top Burg Schaubeck, 13th-century home of Graf Adelmann and Württemberg's most famous estate.

Württemberg's best wines are its reds from the Lemberger (known as Blaufränkisch in its native Austria) and Spätburgunder (Pinot Noir) and various relatives of the latter such as Clevner and Samtrot. These are increasingly being aged in some new oak and cuvées of several grape varieties are becoming increasingly common. The trend toward such blends is a result of strengthening confidence and ambition in red-wine production. This could be said to have begun during the late 1980s when it became apparent to the region's leading winegrowers that whilst Lemberger can easily be coaxed into giving full, substantial red wines, elegance and subtlety are best obtained from other grapes.

Because of its high-profile red wines, few people outside the region think of Württemberg as an important white-wine producer. However, the most widely planted grape in the region is Riesling: it actually covers an area slightly larger than that planted with the grape in the Rheingau, though the respective wines could not be more different. Württemberg's white wines tend to be rounder and more supple than those of the Rhine. Good examples impress more with their rich fruit and herbal-earthy aromas than with elegance or delicacy. The locally developed cross Kerner often gives wines that can match the region's Rieslings, and both Gewürztraminer and Muskateller can give fine aromatic dry wines.

If from a general winemaking perspective Württemberg has a problem, it derives from the Swabians' enthusiasm for their own wines. Regional pride may have blinkered some of the region's growers to the true quality of their product. As a whole the region maintains a solid standard (much higher than some others) but the number of estates and co-operatives currently realising their vineyards' full potential is rather small. Nevertheless there is still more than enough in this charming and occasionally dramatic landscape to fill the itinerary of the discerning wine tourist.

Württemberg

■	●	Wine centre Württemberg
■	●	Wine centre Franken
═══		Autobahn
───		Main road
		Other roads
──		Railway
▓▓▓		International boundary
─ ─ ─		Landesgrenze
----		Regierungsbezirksgrenze

Kür
Oberd
Le
Grossvillar
Knittlinger
Karlsruhe Freudenste
Maulbronn
Ötisheim
Mühlack
Pforzheim
Niefer
Ösche

Below *Besigheim, one of the region's most attractive old towns, is situated between the valleys of the Neckar and the Enz.*

HEILBRONN AND ENVIRONS

RECOMMENDED PRODUCERS

Amalienhof
Lukas-Cranach-Weg 5
D 74074 Heilbronn
Tel: (07131) 251735
Based near Heilbronn the estate's
best vineyard, the wholly-owned
Beilsteiner Steinberg, lies well outside
the town. The Lemberger and
Samtrot can be rich and silky.
Appointment essential Sundays.

**Burg Hornberg (Baron von
Gemmingen-Hornberg)**
D 74865 Neckarzimmern
Tel: (06261) 5001
Young Dajo von Gemmingen runs
this estate which specialises in white
wines. Riesling, Traminer and
Muskateller are the best of a rather
variable range. Appointment
recommended; essential Sundays.

Drautz-Able
Faissstrasse 23
D 74076 Heilbronn
Tel: (07131) 177908
Siblings Richard Drautz and Christel
Able run this fine estate at the edge
of Heilbronn. In addition to the
powerful new-oak-aged 'Jodokus' red
wines they make Germany's best dry
Sauvignon Blanc and some good
dessert wines. Appointment
recommended. Closed Sundays.

HEILBRONN AND ENVIRONS

The city of Heilbronn is one of the two centres around which Württemberg revolves: most of the region's vineyards lie to its east, south and west. The easiest way to reach Heilbronn from the north is via the A81 *Autobahn* from Würzburg; from Baden to the west the A6 *Autobahn* provides the quickest route. However, the most picturesque route is to follow the B37 along the Neckar Valley from Heidelberg. The narrow, winding valley with its densely wooded sides punctuated by small old towns has few vineyards for most of its length, but their absence is more than compensated by its natural charm.

The first vines appear at Binau but they belong to Baden: Burg Hornberg marks the beginning of the Württemberg region. The complex of Burg Hornberg is perched on the pinnacle of a steep vine-covered hillside rising directly from the bank of the Neckar. The estate with its medieval fortifications and 17th to 18th-century buildings has been in the ownership of the Barons von Gemmingen since 1612 and the terraces upon which the vines stand date back even further. The steep terraced vineyards, which are extremely costly to cultivate, are typical of those along Württemberg's river valleys. As mechanisation is virtually impossible a great deal of manual labour is involved – not only in tending the vines but also in maintaining many kilometres of dry-stone walls.

From Binau the road winds past Gundelsheim and its 16th-century Schloss Horneck to the confluence of the Neckar's tributaries the Kocher and the Jagst. Extremely

Above *In Württemberg as elsewhere in Germany Müller-Thurgau is an important grape for everyday drinking wines.*
Above right *Schloss Öhringen, home to the Fürst zu Hohenlohe-Oehringen, crowns the fortified town of Langenburg.*
Right *Vineyards close to Bessigheim in the Neckar Valley.*

picturesque, Gundelsheim is worth exploring as long as expectations of its wines are not too high. White grapes dominate here due to the coolness of the climate, and Riesling can give crisper, fresher wines than it does elsewhere in the region.

Further still to the east lie the vineyards south of Bad Mergentheim in the Tauber Valley. Although the Silvaner and Müller-Thurgau wines from here most closely resemble those of Franken, the other vineyards in the Tauber belong to Baden (Badisches Frankenland).

Fürst zu Hohenlohe-Oehringen
Im Schloss, D 74613 Öhringen
Tel: (07941) 609930
In good vintages Siegfried Röll makes Württemberg's most concentrated dry Rieslings from the estate's Verrenberg site. The reds are mostly traditional in style but the new-oak-aged 'Ex Flammis Orior' is best. Appointment recommended. Closed Saturday afternoons and Sundays.

Graf von Bentzel-Sturmfeder
Sturmfelderstrasse 4
D 74360 Ilsfeld-Schozbach
Tel: (07133) 7829
Small estate concentrating on superior red-grape varieties, especially Spätburgunder. Reds are well made but not spectacular.

WG Grantschen
Winzerstrasse 7
D 74189 Grantschen
Tel: (07134) 98020
Small co-op with a mixed range of wines including some powerful oak-aged reds, 'Grandor' and the bizarrely named 'SM'. Closed Saturday afternoons and Sundays.

GA Heinrich
Riedstrasse 29, D 74076 Heilbronn
Tel: (07131) 175948
Small estate with some promising red wines, many with a well judged touch of oak. Best are the Lembergers and 'GA 1'. Appointment essential Saturday afternoons and Sundays.

Erich Hirth
Löwensteiner Strasse 76
D 74182 Willsbach
Tel: (07134) 3633
Young estate with some good red wines in a forthrightly fruity style. By appointment only.

Kuhnle
Hauptstrasse 49
D 71384 Strümpfelbach
Tel: (07151) 61293
This small estate is a rare source of good-value dry white and red wines in an expensive region. A solid standard. By appointment only.

Gerhard Leiss
Lennacher Strasse 7
D 74189 Gellmersbach
Tel: (07134) 14389
Small family estate with a range of charming, well made dry white, rosé and red wines. Appointment recommended. Closed Sundays.

Staatsweingut Weinsberg
Traubenplatz 5, D 74189 Weinsberg
Tel: (07134) 5040
Good-quality traditional-style and new-oak-aged red wines from the full range of Württemberg grapes. The dry whites are less interesting but of a solid standard. Appointment essential at weekends.

Above *An ancient stepped-gable house in Lauffen.*

Top right *The imperious Schloss Fürst zu Hohenlohe is built around a 15th-century fort.*

RESTAURANTS

Bleichtstuhl
Fischergasse 9, D 74072 Heilbronn
Tel: (07131) 89586
Edgar Rauer's eclectic, unpretentious cooking makes this Heilbronn's best restaurant.

Heilbronner Winzerstübe
Ludwig-Pfau-Strasse 14
D 74072 Heilbronn
Tel: (07131) 84042
Andrea and Theo Menges run this attractive *Weinstube* in the centre of

Heilbronn was almost completely destroyed during the last months of the Second World War but its unique Kilianskirche church remains one of the region's outstanding historical monuments. Most remarkable is the famous tower in which early-Gothic, late-Gothic and Renaissance elements are interwoven. It is decorated with gargoyles that bear more than a superficial resemblance to the diabolical creations of Hieronymus Bosch.

Most of the town is modern and unremarkable but directly outside its suburbs the vineyards begin. Drautz-Able, Amalienhof and Heinrich are the leading producers, Drautz-Able particularly demonstrating the power and substance that Württemberg Lemberger can achieve.

The Sulm Valley just to the east of Heilbronn is home to a large number of the region's best producers. Take the B39 from Heilbronn to Weinsberg below the ruined Burg

Heilbronn. The modestly priced wine list features the wines of the Drautz-Able estate.

Lehenstube
See Hotels: Schloss Lehen.

Schloss Friedrichsruhe
D 74639 Zweiflingen-Friedrichsruhe
Tel: (07941) 60870
Lothar Eiermann runs one of Germany's finest restaurants and country hotels in this baroque hunting lodge dating from 1712. His modern cooking is strongly rooted in French *haute cuisine*. Superlatively comfortable hotel, but be prepared to pay for such excellence.

Zirbelstuben/Hotel Victoria
Poststrasse 2–4
D 97980 Bad Mergentheim
Tel: (07931) 5930
This stylish medium-sized hotel is best known for its excellent restaurant. Adventurous modern cooking and friendly service are complemented by a superb international wine list. Moderate prices in the hotel and restaurant.

HOTELS

Astron
Sulmstrasse 2, D 74172 Neckarsulm
Tel: (07132) 3880
Attractive modern hotel offering fair comfort at a moderate price.

Insel-Hotel
Friedrich-Ebert-Brücke
D 74072 Heilbronn
Tel: (07131) 6300
This comfortable modern hotel is situated on a small island (a park) in the middle of the River Neckar and in the city centre. There are views of vineyards from many of its rooms. Fair prices.

Park-Villa
Gutenbergstrasse 30
D 74074 Heilbronn
Tel: (07131) 95700
This small hotel in an imposing villa has stylish modern rooms and moderate prices.

Schloss Friedrichsruhe
See Restaurants.

Schloss Lehen/Lehenstube
Hauptstrasse 2
D 74177
Bad Friedrichshall-Kochendorf
Tel: (07136) 4044
The rooms in this 16th-century moated castle have remained unchanged for centuries. Chef Freidheinz Eggensperger's sophisticated, creative cuisine makes the stylish restaurant superlatively good. Moderate hotel and restaurant prices.

Hotel Victoria
See Restaurants: Zirbelstuben.

Weibertreu where one of Germany's oldest wine schools is based. The school was founded as the Königliche Weinbauschule in 1868 by Karl von Württemberg. Today it enjoys a high reputation not only for its teaching but also as a wine producer. Recently renamed the Staatsweingut Weinsberg, it produces the full range of Württemberg wines and maintains a consistently good standard, particularly at the red end of the spectrum. Next-door Grantschen is home to one of the region's leading co-operatives (called *Weingärtnergenossenschaft* here rather than *Winzergenossenschaft* as elsewhere in Germany; similarly a vineyard is a *Weingarten* or *Wengert* and a winegrower a *Weingerter*). The cooperative's new-oak-aged 'Grandor' is widely regarded as one of the region's top red wines.

A couple of villages further along the valley in Willsbach, Erich Hirth makes a completely different, vividly fruity style of red wine without any new wood. A few kilometres further brings you to Löwenstein and its ruined medieval castle. This marks the end of the Sulm Valley vineyards and the beginning of the Löwenstein Mountains.

From here follow the back roads (via Eschenau and Bretzfeld) to Verrenberg and the wholly-owned Verrenberg vineyard of the Fürst zu Hohenlohe-Oehringen. Magnificent cellars with wooden casks many centuries old lie beneath the 16th-century Schloss of Öhringen a few kilometres away. Riesling is the principal grape, followed by the usual range of reds. The Fürst zu Hohenlohe-Oehringen also owns the Wald and Schlosshotel Friedrichsruhe, a grand country-house hotel which houses one of Germany's great restaurants. Even without the wines or the historic towns of Öhringen and Neuenstein, the superlative Schloss Freidrichsruhe would be reason enough to make a detour in this direction.

HEUCHELBERG AND STROMBERG

RECOMMENDED PRODUCERS

Dautel
Lauerweg 55
D 74357 Bönnigheim
Tel: (07143) 21719
Ernst Dautel founded his small estate
in 1978 and already his new-oak-
aged Spätburgunder and Lemberger
are the region's finest reds. The dry
Rieslings are also excellent. Strictly by
appointment only.

Graf von Neipperg
Im Schloss
D 74190 Schwaigern
Tel: (07138) 5081
This medium-sized estate consistently
produces traditional-style red wines,
dry whites and dessert wines.
Riesling and Lemberger are the most
important grapes but the Muskateller
and Traminer whites are also first
class. Appointment recommended.
Closed Saturday afternoons and
Sundays.

HEUCHELBERG AND STROMBERG

The heart of Württemberg is the broad expanse of hill country between Heilbronn and Ludwigsburg, divided by the north-south 'axis' of the Neckar's course. The western half of the region is dominated by the Heuchelberg and Stromberg hills. Here the best vineyards lie on the south-facing slopes sheltered by the forested hilltops above them and on the terraced slopes of the Neckar Valley.

Vineyards are only one element of this unspoilt rural landscape. Although there may be few outstanding historical monuments, there is a wealth of fine old buildings in many of the towns and villages that lie between the forest, fields and vines.

On the slopes of the Heuchelberg the leading estate is that of Graf von Neipperg in Schwaigern, reached by talking the B293 west from Heilbronn. The family's vineyards lie five kilometres away on the other side of the wooded hilltops of the Heuchelberg (follow the signs to Neipperg).

The Neippergs have played an important role in the development of the region's viticulture since the Middle Ages. Most importantly, shortly after the Thirty Years' War (1618–48) it was they who introduced the Lemberger grape to the region from Austria; theirs was also one of the first estates to plant Traminer in Württemberg. Both varieties continue to play important roles here. The estate's administrative headquarters and its tasting facilities are in Schwaigern but the vineyards are cultivated from Burg Neipperg, the 12th–13th-century Romanesque fortified tower which stands above the narrow terraces of the excellent Schlossberg vineyard. This site has been cultivated by the family as long as the castle has stood.

Just under ten kilometres away is the beautifully preserved town of Bönnigheim. Much of the medieval town wall remains, including the imposing northern gateway tower.

Below *Vineyards near Bessigheim in the Neckar Valley.*

Although its recorded history goes back to the 8th century the present town plan was laid out by the monks of Kloster Bebenhausen during the late-13th century. The oldest parts of the Alte Schloss also date from this period but today it stands very much in the shadow of the baroque Neue Schloss, set in fine period gardens.

Bönnigheim is also home to the region's new winemaking star Ernst Dautel. His estate is less than 20 years old but is already one of Württemberg's quality leaders. Dautel has made his name primarily with modern-style red wines matured in new oak and he has a feeling for elegance and harmony that many of his colleagues throughout the country could learn from. He also makes fine Rieslings from the steep terraced vineyards of the nearby Neckar Valley which are well suited to the grape. Here he is not alone: the cooperative of Lauffen also makes some good dry whites.

Far across at the eastern edge of region close to the B35 lies the former Cistercian monastery of Maulbronn which was founded in 1147. Dating from the 12th–16th centuries this was one of the earliest Cistercian foundations in Germany. The complex with its outbuildings and dependencies (including a mill, a blacksmith and a coopers' barn) all enclosed within a perimeter wall remains virtually unchanged since the secularisation of 1530. Hermann Hesse, a former pupil at the school established here in the Reformation of 1556, describes Maulbronn in detail in his novel *Unterm Rad* (*The Prodigy*), though he makes no mention of the vineyards planted by the monks. The Abbey church's early-13th-century Paradise Porch is the first German example of the Romanesque-Gothic transition.

Maulbronn's Eilfingerberg and Klosterstück vineyards, long acknowledged to be among the region's greatest sites, are wholly owned by the Württemberg'sche Hofkammer estate in Ludwigsburg. The estate's new director and winemaker are striving to make wines that once again are worthy of the sites' renown.

Above *Steep, south-facing slopes on the banks of the Neckar enjoy the twin advantages of prolonged, intense sunlight and heat reflected from the river surface.*

RESTAURANT

Zum Schiller
Marktplatz 5
D 74321 Bietigheim
Tel: (07142) 41018
The cooking at Regine and Burkhard Schorck's restaurant draws on both French and regional traditions. The huge wine list is moderately priced, making the prospect of an evening here very appealing.

HOTEL

Elefanten
Bahnhofstrasse 12
D 74348 Lauffen am Neckar
Tel: (07133) 14135
A small hotel in a half-timbered house in an attractive old wine town just 10km from Heilbronn.

PLACES OF INTEREST

Besigheim
Lying between the valleys of the Neckar and the Enz, this is one of Württemberg's most attractive old towns. The medieval half-timbered Rathaus is of particular note.
Bietigheim
It is worth spending time to explore this well preserved walled town whose important buildings include the Renaissance Hornmoldhaus and 14th-century Unteres Tor gatehouse.

Above *The courtyard and*
(bottom right) *imperious frontage
of Ludwigsburg's 452-room palace.*

HEILBRONN TO LUDWIGSBURG

RECOMMENDED PRODUCERS

Graf Adelmann
Burg Schaubeck
D 71711 Kleinbottwar
Tel: (07148) 6665
Though quality has varied rather in
recent years, sophisticated
winemaker Michael Graf Adelmann's
Brüsselel'r Spitze bottlings are
amongst the region's most serious
dry Rieslings and red wines.
Appointment recommended. Closed
Saturday afternoons and Sundays.
WG Flein-Talheim
Römerstrasse 14, D 74223 Flein
Tel: (07131) 59520
Modest-sized co-operative with
some good dry Riesling and Kerner
whites. Best are the 'Sankt Veit'
bottlings. Closed Saturday afternoons
and Sundays.
Schlossgut Hohenbeilstein
Im Schloss, D 71717 Beilstein
Tel: (07062) 4303
Hartmann Dippon's substantial
Spätburgunder and Lemberger reds
are vinified with little or no new
wood. His dry whites are much less

HEILBRONN TO LUDWIGSBURG

To explore the wine towns and villages to the east of the
Neckar between Heilbronn and Ludwigsburg, leave the
main roads and follow the back-lanes which wind through
the charming countryside.

Just south of Heilbronn lies the small wine town of Flein
which is as famous for its winemaking rebel Robert Bauer as
for its co-operative. Here the white wines show the most class
even though just a few kilometres along the road you are
once again in red-wine country. Beilstein has some of the
best vineyards in this part of the region as the wines of
Schlossgut Beilstein in the town itself and those of
Amalienhof in Heilbronn prove. The Württemberg speciality
Samtrot, a mutation of Pinot Noir, seems to feel particularly
at home here whilst Spätburgunder and Lemberger also give
wines with ample body.

From Beilstein follow the signs to Burg Schaubeck, the
medieval castle close to Kleinbottwar which is home to the
Graf Adelmann estate. The main body of the castle dates
from the 13th century. In spite of the present Graf's modest
description of it as 'a medieval bunker', the castle and its
beautiful English-style garden have a magical quality about
them. The narrow courtyard at the building's heart gives an
impression of timelessness that seems appropriate since
there have been vineyards at Kleinbottwar for at least a
thousand years. In a good vintage the red wines can have
plenty of power and structure; the dry Rieslings rich fruit
and a fresher acidity than is usually found in the region.

Follow the signs from Kleinbottwar to Ludwigsburg, seat of the Herzogen of Württemberg. At the centre of town stands the Schloss whose construction was begun in 1704 in the baroque style. Building continued through the rococo and neo-Classical periods until the early years of the 19th century. All these styles are also represented in its interiors which could easily take days to explore. To the south it is flanked by the baroque Schlosspark and to the north by Favourite Park with its graceful garden pavilion in which Bohemian and Chinese influences are mixed in an extraordinary manner. On the eastern side of the Schloss lies the enchanting Märchengarten or Fairy-Tale Garden, which fully lives up to its name. A short distance away and somewhat dwarfed by the self-conscious grandeur of the town Schloss lies the more modestly scaled Schloss Monrepos. The lake sunk next to it adds to the beauty of what is now the town's most comfortable and stylish hotel.

impressive. Appointment recommended. Closed Saturday afternoons and Sundays.

RESTAURANTS

Le Carat
Schweiberdinger Strasse 60
D 71636 Ludwigsburg
Tel: (07141) 47600
Excellent restaurant combining French, German and Italian influences. Extensive, moderately priced wine list.
Lamm
Hauptstrasse 23, D 71546 Aspach
Tel: (07191) 20271
Country cooking with a French touch and an international wine list: both excellent. Modestly priced.
Symphonie
See Hotels: Adler.

HOTELS

Adler/Restaurant Symphonie
Stuttgarter Strasse 2, D 71679 Asperg
Tel: (07141) 26600
Modern hotel; small, attractive rooms and friendly service. Rich food and a good selection of local and French wines. Moderate prices.
Schloss Monrepos
Monrepos 22, D 71634 Ludwigsburg
Tel: (07141) 3020
Ludwigsburg's finest for style and comfort with prices appropriate to a baroque palace.

Left Scrolled pediments and gilded, filigree signwork offer architectural riches of a different kind in the smaller towns and villages.

STUTTGART, ESSLINGEN AND ENVIRONS

RECOMMENDED PRODUCERS

Gert Aldinger
Schmerstrasse 25, D 70734 Fellbach
Tel: (0711) 581417
Some of the best reds in the area.
The top wine is new-oak-aged 'C',
but Spätburgunder is also good.
Appointment essential Saturday
afternoons and Sundays.

Jürgen Ellwanger
Bachstrasse 21, D 73650 Winterbach
Tel: (07181) 44525
Red-wine specialists Jürgen and son
Andreas are experts in the cautious
use of new-oak ageing. Best are the
Dornfelder, Zweigelt and cuvée
'Nicodemus'. Appointment essential
Saturday afternoons and Sundays.

Karl Haidle
Hindenburgstrasse 21
D 71394 Kernen im Remstal
Tel: (07151) 949110
Leading white-wine specialist whose
best are the dry Rieslings. Some
dessert wines also impress.
Appointment recommended. Closed
Saturday afternoons and Sundays.

Albrecht Schwegler
Steinstrasse 35, D 71404 Korb
Tel: (07151) 34895
Miniature estate making rich, powerful
reds (blends of Zweigelt, Lemberger
and Merlot) including concentrated
'Granat'. Strictly by appointment only.

Sonnenhof (Bezner-Fischer)
Gündelbach, D 71665 Vaihingen-Enz
Tel: (07042) 21038
Some solid Lemberger and
Spätburgunder red wines. Oak can
be too pronounced. Appointment
recommended. Closed Sundays.

RESTAURANTS

Délice
Haupstätterstrasse 61
D 70178 Stuttgart
Tel: (0711) 6403222
Look out for Friedrich Gutscher's
solo performance in the open
kitchen. Huge wine list and very
knowledgeable Sommelier. Closed
weekends. Early reservation essential.

Ochsen
Kirchstrasse 15, D 71394 Stetten
Tel: (07151) 42015
The cooking and wine list are
unashamedly Franco-German in the

STUTTGART, ESSLINGEN AND ENVIRONS

Stuttgart, best known for its engineering industry, is also an ancient wine city whose special character comes from its dramatic contrasts. Alongside its modern architecture the centre also has its share of magnificent historical buildings. Of these the greatest is the 16th-century Altes Schloss. Dominated by three massive round towers, the Schloss' courtyard surrounded by three storeys of arcades is a masterpiece of German Renaissance architecture.

Around the neighbouring Schillerplatz stands a fine collection of old buildings including the Gothic Stiftskirche church, the late-14th-century Stiftsfruchtkasten with its high pointed gables and the Renaissance Alte Kanzlei.

Between Stuttgart and Leonberg lies the baroque jewel of Schloss Solitude in its extensive grounds. It was constructed between 1763-67 as a venue for the Herzog of Württemberg's extravagant celebrations and its style deliberately mimics, in miniature, that of Würzburg's Residenz. Appropriately enough, it now houses a restaurant.

The city's contemporary spirit finds its finest expression in the Neue Staatsgalerie designed by British architect James Stirling. This daring building with its sloping and undulating walls houses an impressive collection of modern art.

*Right and top right Schlossplatz
and the Neues Schloss. The interior
of the Schloss, destroyed by bombs
in 1944, was reconstructed to
house modern offices.*

Schlegel family's country restaurant. Prices fair, reservation recommended.

Speisermeisterei
am Schloss Hohenheim
D 70599 Stuttgart-Hohenheim
Tel: (0711) 4560037
Food, wine and service live up to the restaurant's grand style. Fair prices. Reservation strongly recommended.

Wielandshöhe
Alte Weinsteige 71
D 70507 Stuttgart-Degerloch
Tel: (0711) 6408848
Chef Vincent Klink's cuisine is sophisticated and creative. Sommelier Bernd Kreis is Germany's best. Quite expensive. Early reservation essential.

Zum Hirschen
Hirschstrasse 1
D 70734 Fellbach
Tel: (0711) 9579370
At this new restaurant in a 16th-century house Michael Pauli combines regional, French and Italian influences. Also several attractive hotel rooms. Moderate prices.

HOTELS

Alter Fritz
Feuerbacher Weg 101
D 70192 Stuttgart
Tel: (0711) 135650
Stylish small hotel in turn-of-the-century villa, fair prices for the central location on the Killesberg.

Right *A statue of Schiller by Danish sculptor Thorwaldsen (1839) towers over Schillerplatz.*

Am Schlossgarten
Schillerstrasse 23
D 70173 Stuttgart
Tel: (0711) 20260
Luxury hotel only a few metres from the main railway station. Extreme comfort: commensurate prices.

Theatrepension Hedda Kage
Pfizerstrasse 12, 70184 Stuttgart
Tel: (0711) 240115
The best value in town if your taste is for austere modern design.

Waldhotel Degerloch
Guts-Muths-Weg 18
D 70597 Stuttgart-Degerloch
Tel: (0711) 765017
Attractive hotel in the leafy suburb of Degerloch. Good value.

Waldhotel Schatten
Magstadter Strasse
D 780569 Stuttgart-Büsnau
Tel: (0711) 68670
Medium-sized hotel combining old and new at the edge of Stuttgart. Comfortable but with city prices.

Zum Hirschen
See Restaurants.

PLACES OF INTEREST

Stuttgart Museums
Alte Staatsgalerie
Konrad-Adenauer-Strasse 32
D 70173 Stuttgart
Tel: (0711) 212 5108
Paintings from the Middle Ages to the 19th century. Closed Mondays.

Galerie der Stadt Stuttgart
Schlossplatz 2, D 70173 Stuttgart
Tel: (0711) 2162188
19th- and 20th-century German art. Closed Mondays.

Hegel-Haus
Eberhardtstrasse 53
D 70173 Stuttgart
Tel: (0711) 216 6733
Documents the philosopher's life and works. Closed Mondays.

Mercedes-Benz-Museum
Mercedesstrasse 136
D 70327 Stuttgart
Tel: (0711) 172 3256
Documents a century of production.

Neue Staatsgalerie
Konrad-Adenauer-Strasse 30
D 70173 Stuttgart
Tel: (0711) 212 5108
An extensive collection of 20th-century art. Closed Mondays.

Porsche-Museum
Porschestrasse 42
D 70435 Stuttgart-Zuffenhausen
Tel: (0711) 827 5685
An impressive display of vintage sports cars.

The Kriegsberg vineyard is just a few hundred metres from the main railway station and both the Altes and Neues Schloss. The Swabians love of their region's wines makes these vineyards virtually sacred land in spite of the fact that much of the region's wealth depends on industrial production.

Stuttgart's finest vineyards lie on the right bank of the Neckar around the suburbs of Obertürckheim and Untertürckheim. The latter is also home to the city's leading quality wine producer, Hans-Peter and Christin Wöhrwag whose white wines are already amongst the best in southern Württemberg. Close by in Fellbach is the Adlinger estate whose strength lies in modern-style red wines matured in new oak.

Other important producers are found in the valley of the Neckar's tributary the Rems. To reach them take the B14 out of town in the Schwäbisch Gmünd direction and leave it by the Weinstadt exit. Follow signs for Kernen to reach the Remstal's leading white-wine producer, the

Karl Haidle estate, directly below the ruined Yburg castle. The young estate of the Kuhnle family is in nearby Strümpfelbach. Just under ten kilometres further up the valley lies Winterbach and the estate of Jürgen Ellwanger. Here there is a rare chance to taste the Blauer Zweigelt grape outside its native Austria.

Just south of Stuttgart on the right bank of the Neckar lies Esslingen, one Germany's oldest towns, whose recorded history stretches back to 866. The centre is dominated by four important churches but the twin spires of the Stadtkirche are the most striking feature of the skyline. Parts of this austere monument are Romanesque, most is early Gothic. The Gothic Dominikanerkirche, a jewel-like miniature in comparison, dates primarily from the late-13th century. Whilst the foundations of the Franziskanerkirche St Georg are at least as old, most of what can be seen today dates from the 15th century but lacks the extravagant flourishes of the Frauenkirche with its fine filigree tower and vaulted ceiling.

Part of the town's remaining defences surround the small Burgberg vineyard on a steep incline on the northern edge of the old town. Because most of the town's fortifying wall has long since disappeared it appears as if the structure has been constructed purely to defend the vines! This is just an impression, but one which would be entirely consistent with the Swabians' deep attachment to their wines.

The Alte Rathaus is one of the finest half-timbered Gothic buildings in the country, dating from the early 15th century. The carved wooden pillars on the first floor are well worth a diversion.

Above *Vineyards on the slopes of the Würmlinger Kapelle near Tübingen.*
Bottom *Each row of vines is arranged to take maximum advantage of the vineyard's aspect.*

Weinbaumuseum Uhlbach
Uhlbacher Platz 4
D 70329 Stuttgart-Uhlbach
Tel: (0711) 325718
Small wine museum in a lovingly restored press house. Includes a collection of Roman glassware. Open only at weekends, April to October.
Württembergisches Landesmuseum
Schillerplatz 6, D 70173 Stuttgart
Tel: (0711) 2793400
Documents the region's history from the Stone Age. Closed Mondays.

**TÜBINGEN, ROTTENBURG
AND REUTLINGEN**

RESTAURANTS

Krone
Brunnenweg 40
D 72658 Bempflingen
Tel: (07123) 31083
Marinna and Werner Veit's
restaurant 5km north of Metzingen
offers excellent value for money. Fish
dishes are especially good and the
wine list offers a fine local and
international range.

Schönbuch
Lichtensteinerstrasse 45
D 72124 Pliezhausen
Tel: (07127) 9750
This very popular, ideally situated
restaurant offers diners fine views
of the Schwäbische Alb Mountains.
The international cooking is good
and prices are moderate.

Vinothek en Ville
Oberamsteistrasse 27
D 72764 Reutlingen
Tel: (07121) 330290
Wine bar with international list and
good simple food.

*Below The riverside setting of
Tübingen attracts many visitors.
On summer nights the river is
alive with lantern-lit boats.*

TÜBINGEN, ROTTENBURG AND REUTLINGEN

Württemberg's most southerly vineyards lie around the
towns of Tübingen and Rottenburg in the Upper Neckar
Valley and nearby Reutlingen. Whilst the wines here may
not be anything very special, the architecture of these
towns certainly is.

The most attractive route to Tübingen is via the B27
from Stuttgart through the densely forested Naturpark
Schönbuch (allow at least an hour-and-a-half by car). Six
kilometres before Tübingen itself lies the small town of
Bebenhausen with its imposing former-Cistercian
monastery. The monks who founded it in 1187 chose an
idyllic setting, the wooded hills forming a perfect frame for
the monastery and its fine church. After the Reformation
in 1535 the monastery became a Protestant school and the
extensive Romanesque-Gothic complex has not been
significantly altered since then. The church's filigree tower
dating from the early 15th century is a masterpiece of
medieval stone masonry which gives an extraordinary
impression of transparency and lightness. The 14th- and
16th-century stained-glass windows and the early-15th-
century frescos are also magnificent. Many hours could be
spent exploring the abbey's other buildings.

The old town of Tübingen could hardly have a more
beautiful situation, straddling a long hill above the Neckar.
In the centre of town is the beautiful Gothic Stiftskirche. Its
construction began during the late-15th century and was
completed with the crowning of its tower in 1529. The
church contains the tombs, ornamented with fine 16th- and

17th-century sculptures, of many of the Fürsten von (or Princes of)Württemberg. Close by on the town's market-place is the Renaissance Rathaus of 1435 with its remarkable astronomical clock. The town hall's interior is even more impressive than the façade, the frescos by local painter Jakob Züberlin (1586) being particularly note-worthy. Along the narrow streets and alleys to the north of the Markt there are many attractive half-timbered houses.

Schloss Hohentübingen stands on the site of the original castle, which was first recorded in 1078. The current building dates from the first half of the 15th century and is a grand example of the Renaissance style. From the castle's grounds is a marvellous view over the Neckar and the famous Platanenallee gardens on an island in the river.

Less than ten kilometres to the southwest lies the old town of Rottenburg. Sections of the town walls still remain, including the Klakweilertor gatehouse and bridge on the left bank of the Neckar and the Kapuzinertörleine gatehouse on its right bank. The Dom St Martin cathedral is a mix of medieval and Renaissance architecture, part of the original building having been destroyed in the fire of 1644. The 15th- and 16th-century wall paintings and the magnificent 14th-century tomb sculptures in the St Moritz Kirche are both well worth a detour.

From Tübingen take the B28 to Reutlingen. The most important survivor from the destruction of 1945 is the graceful Gothic Marienkirche which was completed in 1343. In the nearby streets lie several fine houses incorporating elements from the 14th to the 16th centuries.

Above *Tübingen's old market square bustles with life on Mondays, Wednesdays and Fridays.*

Waldhorn
Schönbuchstrasse 49
D 72074 Bebenhausen
Tel: (07071) 61270
Ulrich Schilling's restaurant situated not far from the former Cistercian monastery of Bebenhausen is reason enough to make Tübingen part of any Württemberg tour. Allow time – and a generous budget – to appreciate his complex and subtle cooking.

HOTELS

Domizil
Wöhrstrasse 5–9
D 72072 Tübingen
Tel: (07071) 1390
This extremely stylish modern hotel on the bank of the Neckar enjoys marvellous views of the old town. Moderate prices considering the location.

Krone
Uhlandstrasse 1
D 72072 Tübingen
Tel: (07071) 31036
Behind the century-old neo-Renaissance façade of the Krone is a hotel offering comfort in the traditional style. Moderate prices.

Franken

The culture and wines of Franken could hardly be more different from those of the regions to the west in the Rhine and Mosel Valleys. Surrounded by hill country on all sides, Franken has long developed in relative political and cultural isolation – or independence, depending upon your viewpoint. From 1253 until Napoleonic times when it became part of Bavaria, Franken was an independent principality ruled by the Prince-Bishops of Würzburg. Franconians still retain a strong sense of regional identity.

Franken has always been dry wine country. The region did follow the trend of the 1960s and '70s towards sweet wines but the changes that took place were more those of emphasis than of principle, which says much about how winemakers value the region's traditions. Indeed one could say the same for Bavaria's wine drinkers, who still constitute the main market for Franken wines.

The traditional Silvaner grape still accounts for 20 per cent of all vineyard plantings. Dry, rich and savoury, the wines yielded by the top sites have been compared by Hugh Johnson to Grand Cru Chablis. It was wines of this kind, sold under the name 'Stein Wein', that made the region famous during the late-17th and 18th centuries when many of its architectural glories were constructed. 'Stein Wein' achieved such renown that the dumpy 'Bocksbeutel' (which translates, rather unappetisingly, as 'goat's scrotum') bottle was introduced in 1718 by the Bürgerspital estate in an effort to guarantee authenticity. It is now the standard shape of Franken bottles but has also, ironically, been widely copied around the world. The most familiar example is that of Mateus Rosé.

Müller-Thurgau accounts for almost half the region's vineyards and achieves wines with far more character here than it usually produces in other regions. The relatively recent introduction of inferior modern grape varieties such as Bacchus, Perle and Ortega is now regretted by many of

Left *Vineyards just after the harvest above the small walled town of Somerhausen.*

Top *Local wine in the distinctively shaped Bocksbeutel heaped in Dinkelsbuhl market.*

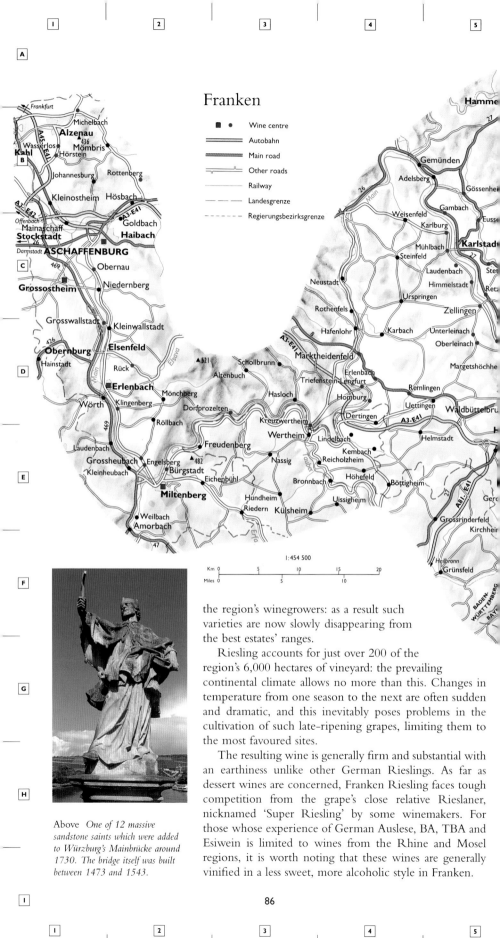

Franken

Symbol	Meaning
■ •	Wine centre
	Autobahn
	Main road
	Other roads
	Railway
– – –	Landesgrenze
- - - -	Regierungsbezirksgrenze

1:454 500

Km 0 — 5 — 10 — 15 — 20
Miles 0 — 5 — 10

Above *One of 12 massive sandstone saints which were added to Würzburg's Mainbrücke around 1730. The bridge itself was built between 1473 and 1543.*

the region's winegrowers: as a result such varieties are now slowly disappearing from the best estates' ranges.

Riesling accounts for just over 200 of the region's 6,000 hectares of vineyard: the prevailing continental climate allows no more than this. Changes in temperature from one season to the next are often sudden and dramatic, and this inevitably poses problems in the cultivation of such late-ripening grapes, limiting them to the most favoured sites.

The resulting wine is generally firm and substantial with an earthiness unlike other German Rieslings. As far as dessert wines are concerned, Franken Riesling faces tough competition from the grape's close relative Rieslaner, nicknamed 'Super Riesling' by some winemakers. For those whose experience of German Auslese, BA, TBA and Esiwein is limited to wines from the Rhine and Mosel regions, it is worth noting that these wines are generally vinified in a less sweet, more alcoholic style in Franken.

At first glance Franken's wine production may seem to be dominated by a few famous estates and several large co-operatives but there are a great many interesting small estates here too. Their low visibility is, paradoxically, often the result of commercial success. The good name which Franken's commitment to tradition has given the region makes it easy to sell good Franken wine for healthy prices. So whilst you may not find many bargains here, there are plenty of tempting discoveries to be made.

ASCHAFFENBURG

 RESTAURANTS

Hessler
Am Bootshafen 4
D 63477 Maintal-Dörnigheim
Tel: (06181) 43030
Chef Doris-Katharina Hessler and
her husband and partner Ludwig
have created from scratch this
remarkable restaurant just east
of Frankfurt. It is definitely a place
for those who enjoy daring
combinations and contrasts of
flavours. Good value when the
cooking hits the mark.

Olmühle
Im Markthof 2, D 63776 Mömbris
Tel: (06029) 8001
Twelve km northeast of
Aschaffenburg. Highly creative chef
Andrej Kuhar is a perfectionist when
it comes to the quality of the
products he uses. A very good
wine list and fair prices.

ASCHAFFENBURG AND ENVIRONS

Most of Franken's best vineyards lie in the Main Valley so the river's course is the best path to follow when getting to know the region's wines. Beginning at the Main's confluence with the Rhine at Mainz, the first vines you find are those belonging to the viticultural island of Hochheim in the Rheingau. The first vineyards of Franken appear almost immediately after the sprawling Frankfurt conurbation.

The simplest route is the A3 *Autobahn* from the southern edge of Frankfurt to Aschaffenburg. Lying close to the Rhine, Aschaffenburg and the stretch of the Main Valley up as far as Miltenberg belonged for centuries to the Prince-Bishopdom of Kurmainz. The town is dominated by the great Renaissance Schloss Johannisburg whose massive red sandstone façade and five towers on the bank of the Main have been the town's hallmark since the building's completion in 1614. The interior has been restored in the early-neo-Classical style of the late-18th century. Today it houses the Schlossgalerie's collection of Renaissance and baroque paintings and the Hofbibliothek library (not open to the public except for occasional exhibitions).

Above *An old inn sign displays the traditional Bocksbeutel bottle of Franken.*
Left *From such a vantage point Aschaffenburg's enchantingly beautiful parks can be enjoyed while at the same time Frankfurt's industrial centres can be glimpsed in the distance.*
Far left *Sunset over the vineyards at Sommerhausen.*

Sonne
Hauptstrasse 2
D 63867 Johannesburg
Tel: (06021) 470077
Eight km to the north of Aschaffenburg, Rita and Friedel Meier run this restaurant in a fine early-19th century country house. Sophisticated cooking at fair prices. The few hotel rooms are pleasant if simple, the location very quiet.

HOTELS

Post
Goldbacherstrasse 19
D 63741 Aschaffenburg
Tel: (06021) 3340
Comfortable, medium-sized hotel in the centre of town close to the railway station. Indoor swimming pool and sauna. Fair prices.
Sonne
See Restaurants.
Die Weyberhöfe
Nahe der B 26
D 63877 Aschaffenburg-Sailauf
Tel: (06093) 9400
Elegant small hotel in a 16th-century country house just 5km from Aschaffenburg. Fair prices.
Wilder Mann
Löherstrasse 51
D 63739 Aschaffenburg
Tel: (06021) 3020
Medium-sized hotel in an attractive 16th-century house in the old town. Moderate prices.

The origins of the Foundation of St Peter and Alexander, a few hundred metres further away and right in the heart of the old town, go back to a Benedictine monastery founded during the 8th century. Much of the Foundation's church and the surrounding buildings date from the 12th and 13th centuries; the late-Romanesque cloisters are especially beautiful. Elements can be found from almost every architectural period up to the beginning of the 19th century when the State of Kurmainz was liquidated by Napoleon.

On the bank of the Main close to Schloss Johannisburg lies the Pompejanum, built by King Ludwig I of Bavaria during the 1840s to display his collection of Roman artifacts. It is a unique example of neo-Classicism, the architect Friedrich von Gärtner having based his plans upon the excavated remains of Roman Pompeii.

Franken's most westerly vineyards lie just to the north of Aschaffenburg and include one of the region's finest, the Hörsteiner Abtsberg, wholly-owned by the Staatlicher Hofkeller estate in Würzburg. This is the warmest corner of Bavaria and its climate, together with the primary rock soil, creates ideal conditions for Riesling.

Above *Anti-bird netting is used to protect Silvaner grapes on the vine at Ochsenfurt.*
Right *Overlapping half-timbered houses line winding streets at Wertheim, situated at the confluence of the Main and Tauber rivers.*

MAIN VALLEY: ERLENBACH TO WÜRZBURG

RECOMMENDED PRODUCERS
Josef Deppisch
An der Röthe 2,
D 97837 Erlenbach bei
Marktheidenfeld
Tel: (09391) 2121
Dry Silvaner and Müller-Thurgau
have good reputations: Traminer and
Rieslaner are specialities.
Appointment essential at weekends.
Rudolf Fürst
Hohenlindenweg 46
D 63927 Bürgstadt
Tel: (09371) 8642
Since taking over in 1975 Paul Fürst
has produced excellent dry Rieslings,
perhaps the most elegant in the
region, and his rich barrel-fermented
Weissburgunders and sophisticated
Spätburgunder reds have written
headlines. The Scheurebe, Rieslaner
and Spätburgunder rosé dessert
wines are also superb. By
appointment only. Closed Sundays.

MAIN VALLEY: ERLENBACH TO WÜRZBURG

The most important vineyards in this part of Franken lie to the south of Aschaffenburg. To reach them take the B469 dual carriageway to Obernburg, at which point you may feel you have been transported back in time.

From Obernburg there is a fine view of the steep vineyards of Erlenbach and Klingenberg (with its ruined Burg) on the opposite bank of the Main. Sadly no one is currently taking advantage of these sites' undoubted potential, though some good wines can be found at the town estate of Erlenbach. At the Rudolf Fürst estate in nearby Bürgstadt, winemaker Paul Fürst demonstrates what the unique combination of geology and micro-climate makes possible. The protection afforded by the hills on all sides makes the small Bürgstadt basin warmer than the great vineyards of Würzburg or the Steigerwald. As a result this is the region's most favourable corner for the production of red wine, particularly Spätburgunder, which at its best resembles lighter red Burgundies such as Savigny-Les-Beaune or Chorey-les-Beaune.

The sandstone soil also helps to produce delicately aromatic white wines, particularly Rieslings, which are less forceful than those made elsewhere in Franken The finest red and white wines made between Erlenbach and Würzburg come from the terraced slopes of the first-class Centgrafenberg site of Bürgstadt. The poor stony soil here makes them slow developers, so patience is recommended. Bürgstadt is now effectively a suburb of the beautiful old

Fürst Löwenstein
Rathausgasse 5
D 97892 Kreuzwertheim
Tel: (09342) 6505
Perhaps not up to past standards but
traditional-style dry Silvaner from the
first-class Kallmuth site is very good.
Appointment recommended. Closed
Saturday afternoons and Sundays.
Städtisches Weingut Erlenbach
Klingenberger Strasse 29
D 63906 Erlenbach am Main
Tel: (09372) 70461
Small estate best known for its
Spätburgunder reds. Mediocre
whites. Appointment recommended.
Closed Saturday afternoons and
Sundays.

 RESTAURANTS

Altes Bannhaus
Hauptstrasse 211
D 63897 Miltenberg
Tel: (09371) 3061
Wolf-Dieter Golze's modern cooking
with some regional touches is
consistently good. Prices friendly. A
few very comfortable hotel rooms.
**Schweizer Stuben/
Taverna la Vigna/Schober**
Geiselbrunnweg 11
D 97877 Wertheim-Bettingen
Tel: (09342) 3070
Andreas Schmitt's Schweizer Stuben
has long been one of Germany's
greatest restaurants. Chef Fritz
Schilling reinterprets Provençal
cooking with pure, intense aromas
and flavours. Sommelier Pedro
Sandvos manages a gigantic selection
of wines. Taverna la Vigna serves
sophisticated Italian food and mostly
Italian wines. Schober offers country
cooking of the highest standard.
Schweizer Stuben is also a small,
extremely stylish modern hotel. Not
surprisingly, you pay for quality here.
Early reservation recommended.
Weinhaus Stern
See Hotels.
Winzerstübchen
Bergwerkstrasse 8
D 63911 Klingenberg
Tel: (09372) 2650
Ingo Holland's extremely creative
cooking makes clever use of Asian
spices. The neighbouring *Weinstube*
offers local cooking at modest prices.

 HOTELS

Hotel Anker
Obertorstrasse 6–8
D 97828 Marktheidenfeld
Tel: (09391) 60040
A small, comfortable hotel with
personal service. Run by the
Deppisch family.

town of Miltenberg, whose origins go back to a fort that
guarded the Roman empire's northern border. Its narrow
streets contain a magnificent collection of 150 half-
timbered houses including the 'Riesen', probably the oldest
inn in Germany. The present building dates from 1590 but
its documented history stretches back to 1411. It is typical
of the region's architectural style in having a ground floor
built of local sandstone.

Continue to Wertheim and follow the valley from here.
The river forms the border between the States of Bavaria
and Baden-Württemberg; Wertheim lies in the latter and
Kreuzwertheim, on the Main's opposite bank, in the
former. Among the town's many beautiful old houses is the
Zobelschen Haus, the narrowest in the region.

Wertheim is best known for Andreas Schmitt's superb
Schweizer Stuben restaurant. Although just over the border
from Franken in a distant corner of Württemberg, it has
always identified itself strongly with the wine region of
Franken (just look at the amazing wine list!). In a region
where gastronomic high points are rather few Schweizer
Stuben, in a quarter of a century of top performance, has
become something of an institution.

The Kallmuth of Homburg is the last of the important
vineyards in this stretch of the valley and the most dramatic.
There is a fine view of it from the A3 *Autobahn* as it crosses
the Main between Wertheim and Homburg. This
precipitous hillside with its massive vine-covered terraces
gives Silvaner wines with a pronounced fruitiness (an
aroma of ripe melons is typical) quite unlike any others in
the region. The Fürst Löwenstein estate of Kreuzwertheim

and Josef Deppisch of Erlenbach bei Marktheidenfeld (not the Erlenbach downstream from Miltenberg) are the leading producers.

At Homburg the Main turns north, snaking its way to Gemünden. Here vineyards reappear and the river turns south-east towards Würzburg. The best vineyards in this stretch of the valley are those of Thüngersheim, whose Riesling and Silvaner wines resemble those of Würzburg but on a lower level.

**Landhotel Schafhof/
Benedikterstuben**
Im Otterbachtal, D 63916 Amorbach
Tel: (09373) 97330,
Restaurant: (09373) 8088
Excellent, quiet hotel 3km outside town in a former Benedictine monastery built in 1720. Moderate prices for this standard.
Schweizer Stuben
See Restaurants.
Weinhaus Stern
Hauptstrasse 23–25
D 63927 Bürgstadt
Tel: (09371) 2676
The attractive rooms, excellent modern German cooking and a superb list of wines from Franken and around the world are all modestly priced in this small hotel and restaurant.

PLACES OF INTEREST

Amorbach
The abbey of Amorbach was secularised in 1803. Owners the Fürsten zu Leinigen then undertook extensive work on the buildings to turn them into a Residenz in neo-Classical style. Several rooms are extremely impressive, most notably the grüne Saal and the library.
Karlstadt
A magnificent late-Gothic Rathaus dates from 1422, its interiors mostly from the early-17th century. Many other fine old buildings lie in the narrow streets that radiate from the market square.
Mespelbrunn
Schloss Mespelbrunn is a beautifully preserved moated castle in late-Gothic and Renaissance styles situated amongst the forested hills of the Spesart.
Schloss Veitshöchheim
The summer residence of the Prince-Bishops of Würzburg lies 7km from the city centre. Vineyards are scarce here as the area is cooler than Würzburg. Originally constructed by Italian architect Antonio Petrini during the 1680s in baroque style, the building's appearance today owes more to the work of Balthazar Neumann who, during the first half of the 18th century, added the side pavilions and imposing rococo staircase and sank the smaller of the lakes with its artificial island.

Top *Pickers take a well-earned break to drink to the success of their Müller-Thurgau harvest.*
Left *Graceful poplars line the riverbank between the town of Ochsenfurt and the Main.*

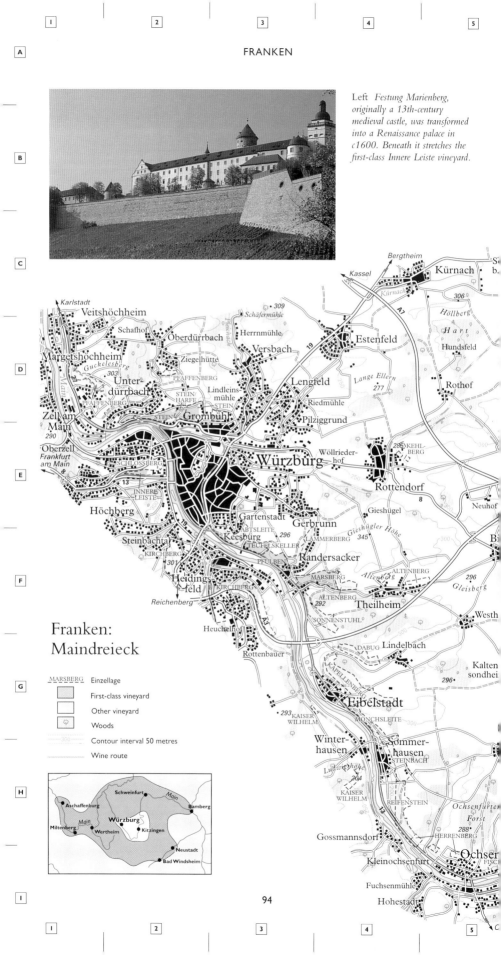

Left *Festung Marienberg, originally a 13th-century medieval castle, was transformed into a Renaissance palace in c1600. Beneath it stretches the first-class Innere Leiste vineyard.*

Franken: Maindreieck

MARSBERG	Einzellage
	First-class vineyard
	Other vineyard
	Woods
	Contour interval 50 metres
	Wine route

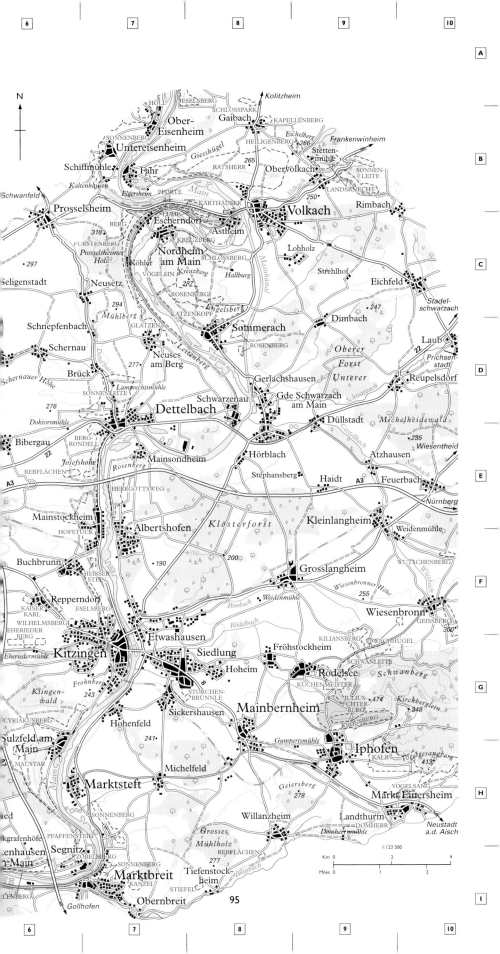

N

Kolitzheim

HOLL IESELSBERG
Ober- SCHLOSSPARK Gaibach KAPELLENBERG
Eisenheim
SONNENBERG HEILIGENBERG Eichelberg 266 Frankenwinheim
Untereisenheim Giesshügel Stetten- SONNEN-
mühle LEITE
Schiffmühle Fahr RATSHERR 265 Obervolkach
Kaltenhausen PFORTE Main 250 LANDSKNECHT
Schwanfeld Elgersheim KARTHÄUSER 250
Prosselsheim BERG Escherndorf Volkach Rimbach
318 HUMP Astheim
FÜRSTENBERG KREUZBERG
• 297 Prosselsheimer SCHLOSSBERG Lohholz
Holz Köhler Nordheim Kreuzberg
Neusetz am Main 282 Hallburg Strehlhof Eichfeld
294 VOGELEIN ROSENBERG Stadel-
Mühlberg KATZENKOPF Engelsberg 247 schwarzach
Schnepfenbach GLATZEN Dimbach Laub
Schernau Neuses Sommerach ROSENBERG 22 Prichsen-
277 am Berg Oberer stadt
Brück Lamprechtsmühle Forst Reupelsdorf
Schernauer Höhe SONNENLEITE Leitenberg Gerlachshausen Unterer
276 Schwarzenau Gde Schwarzach Michelheidewald
Doktorsmühle Dettelbach am Main
BERG- • 235
Bibergau RONDELL Düllstadt Wiesentheid
22 Josefshöhe Mainsondheim Hörblach Atzhausen Sambach
REBFLÄCHEN Rosenberg Stephansberg Haidt Feuerbach
HERRGOTTSWEG A3 Nürnberg
Mainstockheim Klosterforst Kleinlangheim
HOFSTÜCK Albertshofen 200 Weidenmühle
• 190 200 WUTSCHENBERG
Buchbrunn HEISSER Grosslangheim
STEIN Wiesenbronner Höhe 255 Wiesenbronn
Repperndorf Bimbach Weidenmühle GEISSBERG
KAISER ESELSBERG Rödelbach 300
KARL Etwashausen KILIANSBERG WACHHÜGEL
WILHELMSBERGS Fröhstockheim SCHWANLEITE
EHERIEDER Siedlung Rödelsee Schwanberg
BERG Kitzingen Hoheim KÜCHENMEISTER
Eheriedermühle JULIUS 474 Kirchberglein
Klingen- Frohnberg STÖRCHEN- ECHTER- 348
wald 243 BRUNNLE BERG KRONSBERG
CYRIAKUSBERG Sickershausen Mainbernheim
Sulzfeld am Hohenfeld 241 Gumpertsmühle Iphofen
Main KALB 413
MAUSTAL Michelfeld VOGELSANG
Geiersberg Markt Einersheim
Marktsteft 278 VOGELSANG
SONNENBERG Willanzheim Landthurm
PFAFFENSTEIG Grosses DOMHERR Neustadt
Mühlholz Domherrnmühle a.d. Aisch
kgrafenhöfe REBFLÄCHEN 1:123 500
enhausen Segnitz 277 Km 0 2 4
-Main ZÖBELSBERG Tiefenstock- Miles 0 1 2
Marktbreit KANZEL heim
LENBURG STIEFEL Obernbreit
Gollhofen 95

WÜRZBURG

WÜRZBURG

Würzburg is one of the great wine cities of Europe. The magnificence of its great architectural monuments attest to the wealth and power that was concentrated here over many centuries. Wine was always an important element in the culture which revolved around the Prince-Bishops of Würzburg: the Residenz, one of the great masterpieces of rococo architect Balthazar Neumann, symbolises this dynamic combination. Whilst the extravagance and splendour of its Kaisersaal and the ravishing beauty of Tiepolo's frescos are the better known elements, the cavernous wine cellars beneath these rooms (today used as part of the Staatlicher Hofkeller) are no less magnificent.

The Residenz, whose construction took from 1720 to 1744, is framed by extensive gardens, a well preserved section of Würzburg's fortifications and the huge Residenzplatz with its staggering 167-metre façade. It could almost stand as a metaphor for pomp and circumstance – especially the Kaisersaal and the Hofkirche chapel – and a visit here certainly helps to illuminate Franken's culture and history. As far as 18th-century art and architecture is concerned, this great building is deservedly the object of many a pilgrimage. In common with much of the rest of the town, the Residenz was very badly damaged during the last months of the Second World War but it has been painstakingly restored over the succeeding decades.

Before the construction of this huge edifice the Prince-Bishops ruled the region from the massive Marienburg fortress on the opposite bank of the Main. The oldest part of this is the Romanesque Marienkirche which dates back to 706. Construction around the church began in earnest around 1200. These were turbulent times with peasant uprisings in 1308, 1400, 1476 and 1525 and the increasingly extensive fortifications were designed as much to protect the Prince Bishops from their own population as from invaders. Today the fortress houses the Mainfränkisches Museum which has fine collections of Gothic and Renaissance art, including Tilmann Riemenschneider's famous statues of Adam and Eve. It would be easy to spend an entire day exploring the complex. In the Gothic room is the world's oldest functioning clock, which dates from 1350 and there is a magnificent view over Würzburg from the Fürstengarten. Below the Marienburg on the southern side lies the first-class Innere Leiste vineyard, whose wines can be among the region's best.

Return to the town centre by the Alten Mainbrücke which dates from 1133. The baroque sculptures decorating it date from the 1730s and have become another of the city's hallmarks. From here there is a magnificent view of Würzburg's greatest and most famous vineyard, the Stein, which covers a south-facing slope at the northern edge of town almost two kilometres long. It is planted primarily with Silvaner and Riesling, just as it was two centuries ago.

in Iphofen. The wine store is closed Saturday afternoons and Sundays, the *Weinstube* Wednesdays from 11am to midnight.

Staatlicher Hofkeller
Residenzplatz
D 97070 Würzburg
Tel. (0931) 3050920
This very large estate seemed to be hibernating until the arrival of director Dr Rowald Hepp who is working to improve the simple, rather charmless dry wines and the slightly clumsy (but considerably better) dessert wines. The wine store is closed Saturday afternoons and Sundays.

RESTAURANTS

Bürgerspital zum Heiligen Geist
See Recommended Producers.
Haus des Frankenweins
Kranenkai 1, D 97070 Würzburg
Tel: (0931) 57077
The recently restored Balthazar Neumann custom house houses a centre of information concerning the regions' wines, a wine store offering an extensive range of local products and a wine restaurant. The modern cooking is of a solid standard.

Left *One of the 12 baroque statues on Württemberg's Alte Mainbrücke stands before Festung Marienberg castle, once the home of the Prince-Bishops of Würzburg.*

Above *The cellars of the Staatliche Hofkeller lie beneath the 18th-century Würzburg Residenz, one of the biggest baroque palaces in the whole of Germany.*

Right *The baroque-style grand staircase (Treppenhaus) of the Würzburg Residenz, which occupies most of the northern part of the vestibule, is one of the masterpieces of architect Balthazar Neumann.*

Juliusspital
See Recommended Producers.
Rebstock
Neubaustrasse 7
D 97070 Würzburg
Tel: (0931) 30930
Würzburg's best restaurant thanks to Franz Frankenberger's elegant, unpretentious cooking. Rococo architecture and stylish, comfortable rooms. Modest prices in the restaurant and, given its central location, fair ones in the hotel.
Weinhaus Stachel
Gressengasse I
D 97070 Würzburg
Tel: (0931) 52770
Simple wine restaurant in a beautiful old building with an idyllic courtyard. In fine weather there is little chance of a table here without a reservation.

 HOTELS

Maritim Hotel
Pleichertorstrasse 5
D 97070 Würzburg
Tel: (0931) 30530
Large, comfortable modern hotel on the bank of the Main very close to the city centre. Quite expensive.
Rebstock
See Restaurants.
Schloss Steinburg
Auf dem Steinburg
D 97080 Würzburg-Unterdürrbach
Tel: (0931) 93061
This beautiful villa, 6km northwest of the city centre amongst the vines, enjoys wonderful views of the famous Würzburger Stein vineyard and Marienburg fortress. Many rooms are furnished or with antiques. Moderate prices.
Walfisch
Am Pleidenturm 5
D 97070 Würzburg
Tel: (0931) 50055
Small, traditional, family-run hotel with central location close to the Main. Moderate prices.

The limestone soil typical of the region together with an extremely sheltered location results in rich but elegant wines with a pronounced citrus-like fruit. It used to be said that the 'smoky' note in many of these wines came from the trains which passed the foot of the vineyard but since electrification it seems more appropriate to describe this character as 'spicy'. These wines along with a wide selection of other Franken examples can be tasted and purchased at the Haus des Frankenweins nearby on the quayside. A visit to at least one of the town's famous *Weinstuben* is an essential part of any visit to Würzburg.

The old town is dominated by the St-Killian Dom or cathedral which can be reached from the riverbank by the Domstrasse, the scene of Würzburg's daily market during the Middle Ages. Work on the Dom began in 1040 but the plans were revised several times: the decisive period of its current appearance (a mix of Romanesque and early Gothic) was during the late-12th and early-13th centuries. baroque additions were made by Balthazar Neumann. Graves of 39 bishops and aristocratic figures going back to the 12th century are housed within the Dom; a collection matched only by that of the Dom in Mainz.

The nearby Gothic Marienkapelle on the Marktplatz is a miniature masterpiece surrounded by some lovingly restored houses including the beautiful rococo Haus zum Falken. However, for wine tourists the city's Bürgerspital and Juliusspital Foundations will hold even greater fascination. The older of the buildings is the Bürgerspital which has cared for elderly citizens of Würzburg since its foundation in 1319. During the intervening centuries it has accumulated 100 hectares of vineyards which still provide an important source of income for the institution.

The large complex is grouped around a wide courtyard whose ecclesiastical serenity is lightened by the baroque arcade house of 1717–8. In the imposing rooms housing its extensive wine restaurant, however, the atmosphere is far removed from anything ecclesiastical!

The Juliusspital Foundation is only a few hundred metres away. Founded in 1576 by Prince-Bishop Julius Echter von Mespelbrunn, the grandest of its buildings, the baroque Fürstenbau, dates from 1700. Typically for Würzburg the architecture below ground is as impressive as that above. Beneath the 160-metre frontage lies a barrel cellar of equal length which is still in regular use, but the wine estate's offices and cellars occupy only a fraction of this mighty complex which, like the Bürgerspital, is still dedicated to the care of the city's old and infirm. To the residents of both institutions, each of whom receives a daily ration of half a litre of wine, the recent scientific assertion that moderate wine consumption is associated with a lower incidence of heart disease and a longer life expectancy came as no great surprise!

Above *Vineyards above Sommerhausen, whose ancient towers and gatehouses make it a favourite location for artists.*

Below *The main gallery of the Juliusspital barrel cellar extends 160 metres beneath the hospital building.*

MAIN VALLEY:
RANDERSACKER TO
KITZINGEN

RECOMMENDED PRODUCERS

Bickel-Stumpf
Kirchgasse 27
D 97252 Frickenhausen
Tel: (09331) 2847
Small estate, inconsistent quality but
some very clean, fresh dry Silvaner
and Riesling. The estate's restaurant
Zur Weinkönigin serves traditional
regional cooking and is open every
day except Wednesdays from 4pm.
Appointment essential at weekends.

Martin Göbel
Friedhofstrasse 9
D 97236 Randersacker
Tel: (0931) 709380
Good dry Rieslings and Silvaners:
marvellous Silvaner, Traminer and
Rieslaner dessert wines. Good value
in an expensive region. Appointment
recommended, essential Sundays.

Schloss Sommerhausen
Ochsenfurter Strasse 17
D 97286 Sommerhausen
Tel: (09333) 260
Medium-sized estate owned by the
Steinmann family who run Germany's
largest vine nursery. A good general
standard. Auxerrois and
Weissburgunder are specialities.
Appointment essential Sundays.

Robert Schmitt
Maingasse 13
D 97236 Randersacker
Tel: (0931) 708351
This small estate is a bastion of
Franken's dry-wine tradition. Bruno
Schmitt's Rieslings and Silvaners may
have little charm when young but
they develop magnificently. High
quality and moderate prices mean
that many wines sell out quickly.
Appointment essential Sundays.

Schmitt's Kinder
Am Sonnenstuhl
D 97236 Randersacker
Tel: (0931) 708303
Unashamed modernist Karl Schmitt
makes fresh, crystal-clear wines.
Consistently high quality from dry
QbA up to lush Auslese and
Beerenauslese dessert wines.
Appointment essential Sundays.

Josef Störrlein
Schulstrasse 14
D 97236 Randersacker
Tel: (0931) 708281
Small estate founded in 1970. Armin
Störrlein's Riesling and Silvaner are

Right and top right Early
morning tranquility on the
waterfront at Kitzingen.

MAIN VALLEY: RANDERSACKER TO KITZINGEN

The cellars of Würzburg's large estates hold many
impressive wines but the small estates of Randersacker just
to its south offer a positively kaleidoscopic range of
exciting alternatives. Randersacker possesses a row of first-
class vineyards in the form of the Teufelskeller, Pfülben,
Marsberg and Sonnenstuhl which even in Balthazar
Neumann's time enjoyed an excellent reputation. On their
limestone soils Riesling, Rieslaner, Silvaner and Traminer
all flourish, allowing a number of family-owned estates
each to develop their own distinctive style of wine.

To reach the wine town of Randersacker take the B13
southward from Würzburg, a drive of only ten minutes
unless undertaken during the afternoon rush.

It is perfectly possible to spend several days here tasting
one's way through the cellars, and considerably longer
discussing which is the best of the town's many talented
winemakers.

For modern-style wines Schmitt's Kinder, with its
spanking new winery outside the town, is certainly the
leader and for traditional or old-fashioned wines Robert
Schmitt is the number one – but which style is 'better'
depends entirely on personal taste. Where idiosyncratic
dessert-wine specialist Martin Göbel fits into this picture is
no less open to question.

Randersacker is possibly Franken's leading and most
typical wine town. Whilst there are some attractive old

houses in the narrow streets it is not the architecture which primarily impresses here, rather it is the wines in the glass. As diverse as the town's winemakers are, the Silvaners and Rieslings from its vineyards all show a pronounced minerally character and racy acidity that gives them excellent ageing potential.

Follow the B13 the five kilometres southeast to Sommerhausen, whose walls and gatehouses are so beloved of local artists. One of these gatehouse towers houses the unique miniature Torturmtheatre. The Schloss Sommerhausen estate is worth visiting, particularly for its wines from the Pinot family of grapes (including the rare Auxerrois).

The next town, Ochsenfurt, boasts a magnificent early-Renaissance Rathaus, many fine half-timbered houses and an interesting Gothic church. The walled town of Frickenhausen may not have such prominent monuments but gives an even better impression of how towns and villages must have looked during the region's golden age two-and-a-half centuries ago. Here the small estate of Bickel-Stumpf produces interesting dry wines. The town's south-facing Kapelleberg is one of the best sites in this part of the valley.

At Segnitz the river turns north to Sulzfeld, another beautifully preserved old town which is home to the Luckert family's fine Zehnthof estate. Unless you intend to visit the estate take the bridge over the Main at Segnitz to Marktbreit, a town justly famous for its gabled Renaissance Rathaus constructed on a bridge over the Breitbach stream. The town centre could hardly be more picturesque.

fresh and clean, his reds interesting. Appointment essential Sundays.
Zehnthof (Theo Luckert)
Kettengasse 35
D 97320 Sulzfeld
Tel: (09321) 6536
Wolfgang Luckert makes especially good dry Silvaner and Riesling and some impressive dessert wines. Appointment recommended. Closed Sundays.

HOTELS

Wald- und Sporthotel Polisina
Marktbreiter Strasse 265
D 97199 Ochsenfurt
Tel: (09331) 3081
Very comfortable country hotel in forest 2km east of Ochsenfurt on the A3. Moderate prices.
Ritter Jörg
Maingasse 14
D 97286 Sommerhausen
Tel: (09331) 1221
Comfortable small hotel with friendly prices.
Bären
Würzburger Strasse 6
D 97236 Randersacker
Tel: (0931) 706075
Pleasant country hotel with modest prices. The restaurant offers country cooking of a solid standard.

Above *The old wine town of Iphofen, seen from its excellent vineyards.*

STEIGERWALD AND BAMBERG

RECOMMENDED PRODUCERS

Fürstlich Castell'sches Domänenamt
Schlossplatz 5
D 97335 Castell
Tel: (09325) 60160
The history of this aristocratic estate goes back to the 11th century. In spite of a row of solely-owned vineyards sites including the first-class Schlossberg, the estate's dry wines often lack some charm and elegance. However Castell regularly produces spectacular dessert wines. The Weinstall restaurant offers good regional cooking. Closed Thursdays 11am–10pm. The wine store is closed Sundays.

Gerhard Roth
Blüttnergasse 11
D 97355 Castell
Tel: (09325) 373
Small organic estate specialising in Spätburgunder. The reds are amongst the region's best. Good, fleshy Riesling is also produced.

STEIGERWALD AND BAMBERG

In many respects the Steigerwald is an island within Franken. Its different soils (gypsum marl is the norm) and the fine autumns typical here result in highly distinctive wines. Their hallmarks are power, richness and pronounced earthy and herbal aromas.

The Steigerwald's first slopes rise sharply from the undulating country above the Main Valley. Favourably exposed slopes are planted up to an altitude of 400 metres. Where the vines peter out a forest of fairy-tale darkness and density begins whose rich game features prominently in the local cooking. The substantial, even extravagant, architecture in several of the towns and villages adds to an enchanting landscape.

To reach Iphofen, the region's most important wine-growing community, follow the signs from Marktbreit or take the B13 main road to Kitzingen, then the B8.

With 270 hectares under vines, Iphofen produces more wine than any other community in the area. Its first-class Julius-Echter-Berg site gives the quintessential Steigerwald Silvaners and Rieslings which combine depth and substance with a racy acidity that gives even the most concentrated examples a noble harmony.

Each of the gateways punctuating Iphofen's extensive medieval fortifications is of a different design, the famous Rödelseer Tor being perhaps the most beautiful. The Marktplatz is dominated by a three-storey baroque Rathaus and impressive period architecture all around attests to the

Johann Ruck
Marktplatz 19
D 97346 Iphofen
Tel: (09323) 3316
Johann Ruck is rightly well known for his firm, substantial dry Rieslings and Silvaners but his best wines are extraordinary Grauburgunders from old vines in Rödelseer and some highly expressive dessert wines. Appointment recommended. Closed Sundays.

Hans Wirsching
Ludwigstrasse 16
D 97346 Iphofen
Tel: (09323) 3033
Rich yet filigree, Dr Heinrich Wirsching's dry Rieslings and Silvaners from the great Julius-Echter-Berg vineyard are among Franken's finest wines, as are the estate's dessert wines. Even the dry Müller-Thurgau QbAs are beautifully made. Appointment recommended.

Left Ecclesiastical sculpture graces a half-timbered façade in Iphofen. Below The gatehouse of the baroque 'new' Schloss of Castell, home to the family of Fürst Castell.

Above *The village of Castell with its Protestant church (right) amid the excellent Schlossberg Vineyard.*
Right *Its charming sign remains but the first-class Iphofer Kammer restaurant is sadly no longer open.*
Far right *The vineyards of Iphofen bask in the autumn sunshine which gives their wines full-bodied richness.*

RESTAURANTS

Weinstall
See Recommended Producers:
Fürstlich Castell'sches Domänenamt.
Zehntkeller
See Hotel.

HOTEL

Zehntkeller
Bahnhofstrasse 12, D 97346 Iphofen
Tel: (09323) 3062
This fine country hotel housed in
Iphofen's 550-year-old tithe house is
very comfortable and discreetly
stylish. The ambitious restaurant is
quite expensive for the quality but
room prices are moderate.

PLACES OF INTEREST

Ebrach
The extensive buildings of Franken's
first important Cistercian monastery
are almost completely preserved.
The dominant style is baroque, most
of the façades dating from the late-
17th and 18th centuries. The
Abteikirche is a beautiful example of
high Gothic whilst the Klosterkirche
was extravagantly decorated by
Materno Bossi during the last years
of the 18th century.

esteem in which the town's wines were held in earlier centuries. From here follow the signs for Rödelsee, Wiesenbronn and Castell around the foot of the Schwannberg, the Steigerwald's western promontory, to the small winegrowing village of Castell. As the capital of a small principality until its absorbtion by Bavaria in 1806, it has a row of stately (mostly Renaissance) government buildings including a disproportionately large state archive. Inside, records of the wine harvest include the earliest documentary evidence (from 1659) of Silvaner's presence in Franken.

To reach Schloss Weissenstein on the other side of the Steigerwald take the B286 north from Castell and pick up the A3 *Autobahn* direction Bamberg through the Naturpark Steigerwald. Take the Bamberg exit and follow the signs for Pommersfelden.

Schloss Weissenstein, built in white sandstone, is a most dramatic baroque palace and the life's work of Lothar Franz von Schönborn the Prince-Bishop of Bamberg and Prince-Archbishop of Mainz. Like so many other 18th-century rulers of the period he demonstrated his wealth and power through architecture. The massive three-storey staircase sacrifices all practical considerations to grandeur: even the staircase of Würzburg's Residenz pales slightly by comparison. Franz Lothar's descendants, who still live at Weissenstein, open the palace every summer to classical musicians whose work culminates in a week of concerts.

The ancient and historic city of Bamberg nearby is the eastern extremity of Franken's winegrowing region. It is worth visiting more for its architectural riches than for the wine which the few scattered vineyards yield.

The oldest part of the city lies around the great Dom which has been an object of artistic and cultural pilgrimage for more than a century.

The cathedral was first completed in 1012 but fires have razed all trace of it and of its successor. The present building with its four massive towers is primarily Romanesque, dating from the 13th century, and it houses an extraordinary collection of Gothic sculptures and reliefs including the so-called Bamberger Reiter, the depiction of a rider on horseback from 1232–7.

The extensive and beautifully preserved Renaissance Alte Hofhaltung just next to the Dom dates from the late-16th century.

Nearby on a small island in the middle of the Main stands the remarkable Inselrathaus. Bamberg's town hall has stood here since at least the late-14th century. The oldest part of the present building date from the late-15th century, the rest having been remodelled and added during the 1740s and 1750s.

From the right bank of the Main is a fine view across the river of a charming row of old houses known as 'Klein Venedig' or little Venice.

Castell

Protestant since the Reformation of 1559, Castell has a magnificent church dating from the second half of the 18th century. From the outside it looks like a typical large baroque Franconian church but the interior is an austere example of early neo-Classicism.

In this most unusual town, a sense of time different from that in the 'normal' world seems to prevail. For the Fürst Castell family the baroque palace in the centre of the village is the 'new' Schloss, although it was built just over three centuries ago. Just inside the door (entry is strictly by invitation only!) hangs a print showing the cutting and laying of the building's first stone.

MAIN VALLEY: ESCHERNDORF AND VOLKACH

RECOMMENDED PRODUCERS

Michael Fröhlich
Bocksbeutelstrasse 41
97332 Escherndorf
Tel: (09381) 2847
Very reliable producer of dry
Riesling and Silvaner wines which
are invariably clean, fresh and fruity.
Appointment recommended.
Closed Sundays.

Horst Sauer
Bocksbeutelstrasse 14
D 97332 Escherndorf
Tel: (09381) 4364
Small estate with high standards,
particularly for dry Silvaner from
the famous Lump vineyard.
Appointment recommended.

Egon Schäffer
Astheimer Strasse 17
D 97332 Escherndorf
Tel: (09381) 9350
This 3-hectare estate makes
some of the finest dry Silvaners
and Rieslings in Franken but the
combination of quality and scarcity
means that the wines quickly sell
out. By appointment only.
Closed Sundays.

MAIN VALLEY: ESCHERNDORF AND VOLKACH

Follow the signs from Castell to Feuerbach, then to Schwarzach am Main where you take the bridge over the river to Schwarzenau. The small road that runs from here to Escherndorf is a little rough but is worth it for the views of the vineyards. The Main makes a dramatic loop encircling an amphitheatre of vineyards, some of which have a southerly exposure similar to the best sites in the Mosel Valley. The first-class Lump vineyard in the heart of this great slope gives arguably the most sensuous dry Silvaners and Rieslings in the region. Those who generally find dry Franken Rieslings too tart and earthy should try the Lump wines to discover that they can also be succulent and harmonious. Similarly, those who doubt that Silvaner can give exciting wines should be convinced otherwise with the seductively rich wines and their pronounced apricot, melon, and exotic-fruit aromas. Egon Schäffer's tiny estate is foremost, followed by Horst Sauer.

Continue to Volkach, a veritable treasure-trove of old buildings. Much of the town wall is intact including two magnificent gatehouses from the 13th and 16th centuries. Some houses, such as the 15th-century Schelfenhaus, can hardly be appreciated fully because the buildings in the town centre are so tightly packed together.

The market place is dominated by the 16th-century half-timbered Rathaus but the greatest of Volkach's monuments is neither large nor within the town's confines.

Above *Citizens of Volkach mark the completed harvest with an annual Weinfest – period dress is optional!*
Right *The village of Escherndorf celebrates its priorities with a wine festival every single weekend throughout September and October.*
Far right *The delightful medieval town of Volkach is especially rich in architectural interest.*

It is the late-Gothic Maria im Weingarten pilgrimage church situated amongst the vineyards on the Kirchberg. The church houses a marvellous collection of paintings and sculptures including Tilmann Riemenschneider's lime-wood Virgin with Rosary (Rosenkranzmadonna). From the Kirchberg there is also a magnificent panorama which includes Volkach, the vineyards and the Main Valley.

Above: In splendid isolation amid vineyards stands the 15th-century pilgrimage church Maria im Weingarten.

RESTAURANT

Himmelstoss
Bamberger Strasse 3
D 97337 Dettelbach
Tel: (09324) 4776
Herbert Kuffer's cooking is a successful mix of traditional and international influences. Very limited wine list. Modest prices.

HOTELS

Am Torturm
Hauptstrasse 41, D 97332 Volkach
Tel: (09381) 80670
Small, comfortable modern hotel in Bauhaus style right next to one of Volkach's gate-house towers. Moderate prices.

Zur Schwane
Hauptstrasse 12
D 97332 Volkach
Tel: (09381) 80660
Very attractive small hotel in a fine old house with its own (not terribly impressive) wine estate. Friendly prices.

Saale-Unstrut and Sachsen

Two cartographical lines have determined the destiny of Germany's smallest winegrowing regions, the Saale-Unstrut between Weimar, Halle and Leipzig, and Sachsen close to Dresden. The more obvious of the two is the old border between the Federal Republic of Germany and the German Democratic Republic. The other is the 51st degree of latitude, the northern limit – though both regions lie on the 'wrong' side of it – for viticulture in continental Europe.

By the late 1940s both the Saale-Unstrut and Sachsen were on the brink of extinction as winegrowing regions. The effects of the phylloxera epidemic of the late-19th century, then those of economic crises and war, combined to take most of the vineyards out of cultivation. Although winegrowers were able to expand the vineyard area again during the communist period, the development of quality wine production went into reverse. Only during the last few years have growers finally been able to plant the vines they wish, to cultivate the vineyards with purpose-made machinery and to take advantage of the cellar technology that winemakers in the West have long taken for granted.

The continental climate is a hard fact of life for winegrowers in both regions. The warm, dry summers ripen grapes well but late frosts in spring can decimate the vines just as the sudden arrival of winter can dramatically reduce harvest expectations overnight. The one great advantage growers have is an unfailingly warm human climate. The people of Halle, Leipzig and Dresden applaud every achievement of their local winemaking heroes with an enthusiasm unmatched in Germany's other regions. They are also happy to pay prices that make it possible to finance the considerable investments currently under way

Left *The belvedere and formal gardens of baroque Schloss Wackerbarth in Radbeul.*

Top *An old cellar wine restaurant lies beneath this gilded wrought-iron sign in Naumburg.*

Saale-Unstrut
and Sachsen

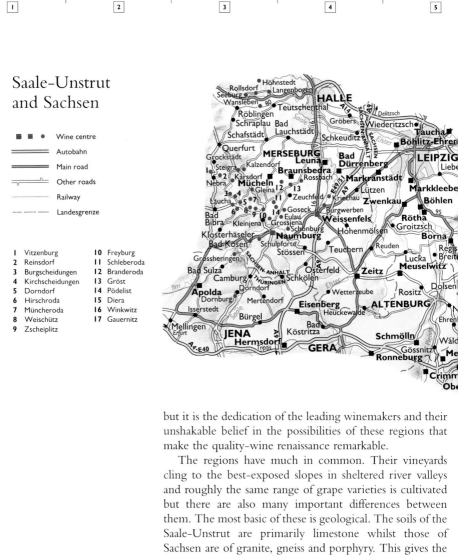

- ■ ■ ●   Wine centre
- ══════   Autobahn
- ▨▨▨▨   Main road
- ━━╜━   Other roads
- ──────   Railway
- ─ ─ ─   Landesgrenze

1	Vitzenburg	10	Freyburg
2	Reinsdorf	11	Schleberoda
3	Burgscheidungen	12	Branderoda
4	Kirchscheidungen	13	Gröst
5	Dorndorf	14	Pödelist
6	Hirschroda	15	Diera
7	Müncheroda	16	Winkwitz
8	Weischütz	17	Gauernitz
9	Zscheiplitz		

but it is the dedication of the leading winemakers and their unshakable belief in the possibilities of these regions that make the quality-wine renaissance remarkable.

The regions have much in common. Their vineyards cling to the best-exposed slopes in sheltered river valleys and roughly the same range of grape varieties is cultivated but there are also many important differences between them. The most basic of these is geological. The soils of the Saale-Unstrut are primarily limestone whilst those of Sachsen are of granite, gneiss and porphyry. This gives the wines of Sachsen a sleeker, more minerally character than that of the the fuller, more juicy wines of Saale-Unstrut. Cultural differences are also important. Sachsen's vineyards lie very close to Dresden – some of the best sites actually lie within its suburbs. This results in a particularly close association of the region's wines with the city's rich culture. Saale-Unstrut is a charming rural backwater by comparison but it is too early to say exactly how these contrasting factors will affect the regions' development.

Both regions share with Franken, the nearest wine-growing region to the west, a strong dry-wine tradition although the climate gives affects their relative degrees of acidity. In the best cases there is more than enough fruit and body to balance pronounced acidity but a great many wines still taste rather thin and sour.

The legacy of misguided vineyard plantings frequently makes itself felt. Many vineyards in both regions will give better wines only when the vine material has been radically improved, which is why extensive replantings are currently under way. The following must therefore still be taken as a report on 'work in progress'.

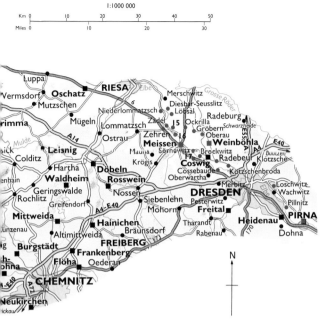

SAALE-UNSTRUT

The origins of viticulture in the valleys of the River Saale and its tributary the River Unstrut go back well over a thousand years.

Slightly cooler than the Mosel Valley but with more sunshine and less rain, the Saale-Unstrut's climate is rather less extreme and continental than that of Sachsen. The climate and the limestone soil which predominates are reminiscent of Franken and the wines also bear a certain resemblance to Franken wines, but when well made Saale-Unstrut wines are more delicate. The best are the Rieslings, Traminers and Weissburgunders, but these grapes require excellent sites in order to ripen fully. Müller-Thurgau and Silvaner, both grapes with limited capabilities, together account for two-thirds of all plantings.

The beautiful old town of Naumburg, founded a millennium ago, is the logical place to start any tour of the region. It is most easily reached by the A9 *Autobahn*, Naumburg exit.

The town is best known for its magnificent Dom St Peter und Paul which was first completed in 1040, but the existing building is a synthesis of the Romanesque and Gothic styles from the 13th century (though the twin East Towers were made higher in about 1500 and gained baroque roofs during the 18th century). The cathedral houses a unique collection of late-Romanesque and early-Gothic carvings including some of the earliest depictions of common people in German art, which offer a rare insight into the life of this distant period.

The tower of the Gothic church of St Wenzel has a 72-metre-high viewing platform which gives the finest view

Top *Schloss Neuburg overlooks Freyburg in the Unstrut Valley.*
Above *The narrow back streets of Naumburg, founded in 1010, offer every kind of architectural curiosity.*

SAALE-UNSTRUT

RECOMMENDED PRODUCER

Lützkendorf
Saalberge 31
D 06628 Bad Kösen
Tel: (034463) 61000
Udo Lützkendorf and his son Uwe
run easily the best estate in the
Saale-Unstrut. Their finest wines are
the racy dry Rieslings from the
Pfortener Köppelberg and the subtly
aromatic, silky Traminers from
Freyburg. In their Strausswirtschaft
(open daily from 10am–8pm) you
can sample their wines and home-
made traditional sausages.
Appointment recommended for
tastings.

Below *'Sächsisohe Schweiz' or
'Sachsen's Switzerland' along the
River Elbe upstream of Pirna.*

of the Dom. In the Marktplatz, the heart of town, the Renaissance Rathaus with its round gabled frontage is very striking. In common with most of the buildings here it dates from the years immediately after the great fire of 1517 which destroyed much of the town. From the Rathaus radiates a network of narrow streets and alleyways full of fine houses from the 15th–18th centuries.

From Naumburg it is only a short drive to the former Cistercian monastery of Kloster Pforta. Founded around 1100, the monastery played an important a role in the development of the region's viticulture just as the great monasteries of the Rheingau did during the same period. In 1154 the monks planted the Köppelberg vineyard which to this day is regarded as one of the region's finest sites. The abbey now houses the State winery which, sadly, does not fulfil its intended function of giving quality leadership in the region.

A shining example is however provided by the small Lützkendorf estate of nearby Bad Kösen. This attractive small spa town, situated between wooded and vine-covered hills in the Saale Valley, is famous for its salt works which were constructed on the orders of August the Strong in 1723 in an effort to guarantee Sachsen's independence from Prussian salt. A short distance upstream lie the ruined

Left *The 'Steinernes Bilderbuch'
or stone picture book, carved near
Freyburg by an unknown
18th-century artist.*

RESTAURANTS

Altdeutsche Weinstuben zum Künstlerkeller
Breite Strasse 14
D 06632 Freyburg
Tel: (034464) 27292
These cellars, in which local artists
exhibit their work, have housed a
wine restaurant for more than a
century. In 1992 a small, moderately
priced hotel was added.

Lützkendorf
See Recommended Producer.

Restaurant and Hotel Zur Alten Schmiede
Lindenring 36–37
D 06618 Naumburg
Tel: (03445) 208161
The region's best restaurant is in a
recently restored old house that
once contained a forge, elements of
which have been retained. Regional
cooking with a light modern touch.

HOTELS

Rebschule
Ehrauberge 33
D 06632 Freyburg
Tel: (034464) 27647
Small hotel idyllically situated among
vines just above the town.

Stadt Aachen
Markt 11
D 06618 Naumburg
Tel: (03445) 2470
New hotel housed in three fine
old houses on Naumburg's historic
marketplace. Comfortable modern
rooms and moderate prices.

Unstruttal
Markt 11
D 06632 Freyburg
Tel: (034464) 7070
Pleasant small hotel in the centre
of the old town.

Villa Ilske
Ilskeweg 2
D 06628 Bad Kösen
Tel: (034463) 27363
Attractive, fairly comfortable small
hotel in a recently restored 1915
villa. A quiet location with fine views
of Bad Kösen and environs.
Modest prices.

Zur Alten Schmiede
See Restaurants.

Zum Wehrdamm
Loreleypromenade 3
D 06628 Bad Kösen
Tel: (034463) 28405
Small, modestly priced family-run
hotel.

castles of the Rudelsburg and Burg Saaleck, close to the
only significant vineyard of the Ilm Valley and the State of
Thüringen, the Sonnenberg of Grossherringen.

Most of the region's vineyards lie in the valley of the
Unstrut where, on the river's left bank, there are many
well-exposed southwest-facing slopes. To reach this area
follow the signs from Naumburg, direction Freyburg.

The first important winegrowing community is
Grossjena in whose fine Sonneck vineyard stands one of
the region's most remarkable historical monuments.
During the 18th century an unknown artist carved a series
of reliefs which have since been known as the 'Steinernes
Bilderbuch' or stone picture book.

From here it is only a short distance to the old town of
Freyburg. It nestles at the foot of the steep terraces of the
Edelacker vineyard which is crowned by Schloss
Neuenburg. The castle was built between 1090 and 1127
by the Dukes of Thüringen but remodelled during the
late 16th and 17th centuries. Its restoration has been
completed only recently. The 'Dicken Wilhelm' tower
houses the Schloss museum which documents the region's
history.

The town itself is dominated by the twin towers of the
Marienkirche church which, like the Dom of Naumburg,
mingles elements of Romanesque and Gothic styles.
Freyburg is also home to the region's cooperative winery
whose wishy-washy wines, sadly, cannot be recommended.
The Rotkäppchen Sekt company was established in
Freyburg in 1856 but it now makes its cheap sparkling wines
almost exclusively from imported base wines. Its cavernous
cellars with the 160,000-litre cuvée barrel speak of the
glories of an age before the catastrophes of the 20th century,
from whose legacy the region is finally freeing itself.

Above *Terraced vineyards by the River Elbe southeast of Meissen.*

SACHSEN

PLACES OF INTEREST

Pirna

The 15th–17th century fortress of Sonnenstein stands on a rocky plateau above the small town of Pirna and was a vital stronghold until the early-18th century. The late-Gothic Rathaus and many fine Renaissance houses around the Marktplatz show how wealthy this trading town once was. The late-Gothic Marienkirche church possesses a magnificent carved altar from 1616 and the 14th-century Dominican Klosterkirche has a fine Gothic painted vaulted ceiling.

Sächsiche Schweiz

The most spectacular section of the Elbe Valley, between the German-Czech border and the town of Pirna just south of Dresden, earned the name 'Sachsen's Switzerland' centuries ago. Massive and bizarrely formed sandstone cliffs tower over the river's winding course in this national park. You might not need mountaineering skills to scale the Lillienstein, Königstein or Pfaffenstein but you will need to be reasonably fit and to wear a pair of good

SACHSEN

A pioneering spirit amongst winegrowers is something usually associated with the New World, though even there regions such as the Napa Valley in California and the Barossa Valley in Australia can look back at well over a century of winemaking tradition. Such a spirit is so much less familiar in the heart of Europe that it is not always immediately recognisable, but there can be no doubt that it exists in Sachsen.

Although the history of viticulture here goes back to the Middle Ages, during the half century preceding the fall of the iron curtain on November 9, 1989 the quality-wine industry was eroded to the point of non-existence. Wine continued to be produced, indeed during the Democratic Republic years the area under vine expanded from less than 50 hectares to 300 hectares at the end of the 1980s. Wines that were better than merely drinkable, however, were rare.

During this period the Meissen cooperative and Landesweingut (today Staatsweingut) Schloss Wackerbarth dominated the region's wine production, but neither establishment was in a position to pursue high-quality goals owing to their organisation and lack of materials and equipment. Wine culture effectively ceased to exist and traditions of quality-wine production going back to at least the first decades of the 18th century were lost.

The result is that since 1989 the region's winegrowers have had to start with a virtually clean slate. The fact that so many fallow vineyards have been brought back into cultivation by private initiative during the last decades says much about the regional character – there are more than 2,000 vineyard owners in Sachsen in spite of their being only 340 hectares of vines. This illustrates perfectly how the development of a wine industry and the culture associated with it depend upon the prevailing sense of national identity.

The fact that the restoration of Dresden's historic monuments was undertaken in spite of communist doctrines is an unmistakable expression of the Sachsens' regard for their heritage. To put this is into perspective it is worth comparing the events in East Berlin and Dresden during the early 1950s. Whilst the communist authorities in Berlin decreed the destruction of the Berlin Stadtschloss and Wilhelmstrasse (the equivalent of Whitehall in London), those in Dresden began the painstaking reconstruction of their historic city – including the monuments associated with its royal past.

The comparison between Berlin and Dresden is a natural one since they are the capitals of two States, Prussia and Sachsen, which are historic rivals. Ask a non-German to name a German State and he or she will almost certainly answer Prussia. For most people inside and outside Germany the power and wealth of Sachsen during the 18th century has been overshadowed by Prussia's rise to power during the 19th century, but it can be argued that Prussia's rise was at Sachsen's expense. Sachsen had allied itself with Napoleon in 1806 and at the Vienna Congress of 1815 it lost two thirds of its territory to Prussia. Sachsen's political power went into decline and Prussia's slow rise began to the position of dominance it had achieved by 1871.

Above *A clipped yew avenue leads to baroque Schloss Wackerbarth in the Dresden suburb of Radebeul.*

Below *The rocky vineyards of Diesbar Seusslitz just north of Meissen.*

walking boots. Breathtaking views make the effort more than worthwhile. For the less energetic, steamers regularly ply this part of the Elbe Valley. Allow a full day for such an excursion. If you have limited time but are determined to have at least a taste of adventure, the Kiknitzschtal Gorge can be reached using a small tram-like railway that runs from the attractive spa town of Bad Schandau on the Elbe. The Obere Schleuse (where refreshments are available) offers some of the most ravishing scenery in Sachsen and the climb to the Königsplatz viewing point is not too demanding.

Schloss Moritzburg

The massive baroque palace of Moritzburg 18km northwest of Dresden was built by August the Strong as a hunting lodge. Designed by MD Pöppelmann and constructed between 1723–36, an extensive lake was sunk alongside it and a 5km-long tree-lined avenue laid out in the direction of Dresden. Today the palace houses a baroque museum whose furniture and porcelain collections are particularly impressive.

During the period before these developments the city and State played a major political, economic and cultural role in Europe. During August the Strong's rule (1694–1733) Sachsen became a major European power and Dresden became one of the continent's cultural centres. Great monuments such as the Zwinger, Hofkirche, Taschenberg Palais and Japanisches Palais in Dresden, the Mortzburg hunting castle and Schloss Pillnitz in the surrounding area document this power: in the same way that the Notre Dame, the Arc de Triomphe and the Eiffel Tower make Paris such a focus for French national pride, these masterpieces of baroque architecture make Dresden the focus for the pride of Sachsen.

It was this pride – together with a healthy appetite for wine – which during even the darkest days of the communist period moved the people of Sachsen to fell trees, clear bushes and painstakingly rebuild walls in order to replant abandoned vineyard terraces in the Elbe Valley. Even if some of this work was not undertaken as professionally as it might be today, it provided the essential basis for the region's return to the European wine stage.

For anyone who has travelled through the wine regions of Europe it is not difficult to recognise the tremendous potential of Sachsen's vineyards. The precipitous concertina folds of the Goldener Wagen terraces mark it out as a special place for the vine. Similarly, the undulating slope of the Königlicher Weinberg framing the Weinbergskiche

church leave no doubt that it must be possible to grow remarkable wines here. If proof were needed that great wines were once made in Sachsen, a local winegrower recently showed me an almost perfectly preserved bottle of wine from the Königliche Weindomäne made in 1718 and bearing the seal of August the Strong. At this time the bottling of wine was a very exceptional practice, considered worthwhile only when the wine was of truly remarkable quality. Descriptions in 18th-century wine literature strongly suggest that the finest wines of this period were comparable with the naturally sweet Auslese of today. The grapes used for such wines were almost certainly Traminer, whose special bouquet made it the only variety to be cultivated as a monoculture at the time.

The winegrowers of the region draw their inspiration not only from their own history but also from their colleagues in winegrowing nations as diverse as Austria and America. If great wines are soon to be made once again in Sachsen, they will be not be copies of past glories, but a new interpretation of the possibilities that nature makes possible here. In Sachsen the finest wines of recent vintages, the products of young winemakers still gaining experience and experimenting, make the future of winemaking seem auspicious indeed. With a little luck it will not be many years before Sachsen will have to be taken seriously not just because of its artistic and musical achievements, but also for its achievements in winemaking.

Bottom left and below *Meissen, which boasts some of the finest vineyards in Sachsen, grew up beneath a fortress built in 929 by King Heinrich I. Substantial architecture reflects the prosperity the town has enjoyed since the 18th century when its porcelain achieved worldwide recognition.*

Above *The grandeur of Dresden's monuments – the Semper Opera and Hofkirche, the Zwinger palace, the Schloss, Albertinum, Japanisches Palais and so many more – cannot fail to impress even the most jaded traveller.*

DRESDEN

RECOMMENDED PRODUCERS

Weinbau Friedrich Aust
Weinbergstrasse 10
D 01445 Radebeul
Tel: (0351) 8301454
The Aust family's miniature estate already produces some of Sachsen's best wines including a dry Traminer from 65-year-old vines in Radebeul's Goldener Wagen site.

Weinbau Klaus Seifert
Weinbergstrasse 26
D 01445 Radebeul
A tiny estate producing very clean, fruity dry wines. There is no telephone but Herr Seifert is best caught in the late afternoon.

DRESDEN

It is not widely recognised that Dresden is a great wine city. Some of the finest of Sachsen's 325 hectares of vineyards lie within its boundaries including the Goldener Wagen of Radebeul and the Königlicher Weinberg of Pillnitz, whose name illustrates the importance attached to winemaking by the Sachsen Royal Family. At the height of their power during the 18th century, five times the present area was under vine. Contemporary descriptions of the wines and rare surviving examples attest to a highly developed wine culture. Although a variety of factors have since conspired to reduce the number of vineyards dramatically, the Sachsen people's interest in their wines remains intense.

The grandeur of the city's monuments is intact thanks to the painstaking restoration which has taken place since the city's destruction by British bombs in February 1945. Decades of work on the Schloss are now approaching completion and the Frauenkirche church is miraculously arising from the heap of rubble it remained for nearly 50 years.

This is not the first time Dresden has been rebuilt. The Prussian bombardment of 1760 and the great fire of 1685 were hardly less devastating than the air raids of 1945.

Any tour of the city should begin at the Altmarkt: the large piazza has probably been the centre of town since its foundation eight centuries ago. On its eastern side stands the fourth incarnation of the Kreuzkirche, constructed after the destruction of its predecessor in 1760 and radically restored during the early 1950s. The monumental austerity of its remodelled interior seems to capture perfectly the spirit of those years, and it is certainly one of Germany's greatest pieces of 20th-century ecclesiastical architecture.

Ranged about the nearby Neumarkt are Dresden's Art Academy; the Albertinum Museum with its fine collection of paintings by Romantic master Caspar David Friedrich and modern German art; the Transport Museum and the fascinating Frauenkirche reconstruction site. Climb the steps to the Brühlsche Terrasse with its magnificent view over the river: standing here it is easy to understand why Dresden was dubbed 'Florence on the Elbe'. Follow the terrace along to Augustusbrücke and facing the bridge you will see the Schloss and the wonderful baroque Kathedrale or Hofkirche of 1739–55 with its soaring 85-metre spire. The spire of the schloss has been reconstructed only recently and now dominates the skyline as it did when

Above *The Semper Opera, named after its architect Gottfried Semper, dates from 1871–8. It has been the scene of many important premières including several operas by Richard Strauss.*

Staatsweingut Schloss Wackerbarth
Im Schloss, D 01445 Radebeul
Tel: (0351) 722728
With over 100 hectares of vineyard this is easily the region's largest estate but few of its wines rise above mediocrity. The best bets are the dry Grauburgunders and Weissburgunders. Closed Sundays.

Klaus Zimmerling
Bergweg 27, 01326 Dresden-Pillnitz
Tel: (0351) 2811608
Small estate run by former engineer Klaus Zimmerling. Highly individual hand-crafted wines. The sophisticated dry Riesling, Traminer and Grauburgunder are the region's best wines. By appointment only.

RESTAURANTS

Ars Vivendi
Bürgerstrasse 14
D 01127 Dresden
Tel: (0172) 3486768
Dieter Brüning's imaginative cooking
may strike some as eccentric but his
creations are full of colour, aroma
and flavour. A good international
wine list and moderate prices.

Carousel
See Hotels: Bülow Residenz.

Erholung
Rissweg 39
D 01324 Dresden-Weisser Hirsch
Tel: (0351) 377993
Mario Pattis, chef of this stylish new
restaurant is extremely talented. He
could even occasionally be accused
of trying a little too hard. The street-
plan of Dresden painted on the
ceiling provides an interesting
diversion. Moderate prices.

Kahnaletto
Am Augustusbrücke
D 01067 Dresden
Tel: (0351) 4953037
A small restaurant plum in the centre
of town right next to the Augustus
bridge and the Semper Opera. Chef
Peter Glöckner offers light modern
cooking with an Italian touch.

Below *The Langer Gang, 22
Tuscan arcades enclosing a stable
courtyard, is an elegant feature of
the Renaissance Schloss.*

Canaletto painted here over 200 years ago. The Grüner Gewölbe, King August the Strong's collection of jewels and extravagant ornaments, will soon be returned to the cellar of the Schloss from their temporary home in the Albertinum museum.

Next door stands the Taschenbergpalais, once the city residence of August the Strong's mistress Constantia von Cosel – note the covered walkway connecting the buildings! It is now Dresden's sublime new Kempenski hotel. The neighbouring Zwinger complex, a masterpiece of German baroque, was designed by MD Pöppelmann for August the Strong between 1711 and 1728 and was used primarily for state celebrations. Works now exhibited in the Zwinger include several rooms of Canaletto's paintings of Dresden and environs and a row of superb Rembrandts, as well as August the Strong's porcelain collection. The masterful reconstruction work on the nearby Semper Opera was finally completed in 1985.

From the Augustusbrücke bridge there are magnificent views of the city's principal monuments. On the right bank of the Elbe stands the famous golden statue, erected in 1736, of August the Strong on a rampant horse and the huge Japanisches Palais which he built to house his porcelain collection.

Here begins the Neustadt district of Dresden, many of whose narrow streets seem to have remained unchanged for untold decades. The Neustadt suffered less severely from the destruction of February 1945 and the decades of communist rule. For many years it was the centre of the city's art scene, and since German reunification the district has blossomed. If Dresden is able to rival Berlin as a cultural

HOTELS

Bülow Residenz/ Restaurant Carousel

Rähnitzgasse 19
D 01097 Dresden-Neustadt
Tel: (0351) 44033
Ralf J Kutzner is director of
Dresden's most exquisite hotel and
chef in its finest restaurant. The
painstakingly restored house dates
from 1730 and is one of many fine
old houses in this corner of
Dresden's Neustadt. The stylish
restaurant offers refined but
unpretentious international cuisine.
and an excellent selection of local
and international wines. In summer
a table in the courtyard with its vine-
covered pergolas is a delight. Prices
are moderate in the restaurant but
fairly expensive in the hotel.

Kempinski Taschenbergpalais

D 01067 Dresden
Tel: (0351) 49120
This magnificent hotel, recently
opened right next to Dresden's great
monuments, offers the ultimate in
style and luxury. The 1709 baroque
palace was once the city home of
August the Strong's mistress
Constantia von Cosel: before you
enter be prepared to pay your share
towards the cost of its restoration!
As yet the restaurant cannot match
the hotel's high standards.

Schloss Eckberg

Bautzner Strasse 134
D 01099 Dresden-Weisser Hirsch
Tel: (0351) 52571
Romantic hotel in one of Dresden's
so-called Wein Schlösser. The
extravagant neo-Gothic building
stands in a large and wonderful park
above the Elbe. Quite expensive.
The restaurant has apparently
improved recently.

centre once again, then this is in no small measure owing to the vitality of the Neustadt.

Perhaps the greatest surprise for first-time visitors is the architectural richness of many districts outside the city centre. Take the Käthe-Kollwitz-Ufer along the left bank of the Elbe to Blasewitz and you will find street after street lined with grand turn-of-the-century villas. On the way there is a breathtaking view of the three so-called Wein Schlösser on the opposite bank of the river: Albrechtsberg, Stockhausen and Eckberg, in that order as you pass them. From Blasewitz the 'Blaue Wunder' or Blue Wonder suspension bridge gracefully spans the river to the noble suburb and artists' colony of Loschwitz. Here among a marvellous collection of fine, mostly late-19th century houses, many of members of Dresden's dynamic artistic community live and work.

Follow the Pillnitzer Landstrasse past the funicular railway that climbs the steep hillside above the river to Wachwitz. The Rhododendron Park here is reason enough to travel to Dresden in the spring. Next to Pillnitzer Landstrasse stands Wachwitz' vineyard, part of the Königlicher Weinberg. A short distance further along the main road is Pillnitz with its ravishing baroque palaces Wasserpalais and Bergpalais (Schloss Pillnitz). They were built as country residences for Constantia von Cosel who took a great interest in the vines that belonged to them. The beautiful terraced vineyards of the Königlicher

Above and bottom right
Inspiration for the design of the Bergpalais Schloss Pillnitz was drawn both from French baroque and from the lavish oriental motifs which decorate August the Strong's porcelain collection.

Schöner Aussicht
Krügerstrasse 1
D 01326 Dresden-Loschwitz
Tel: (0351) 36305
Small hotel with simple if pleasant rooms that offer good value for money in an expensive city.

Weinberg (replanted during the early 1980s) frame the elegant Weinbergskirche which was built at the same time as the Schloss. In the garden is the world's oldest camellia, which is protected by an extraordinary hi-tech greenhouse.

In part of the cellars of Schloss Pillnitz, which date from the late 16th century, Klaus Zimmerling makes the region's finest wines. To reach his estate and vineyards take the narrow Bergweg past the main body of the Königlicher Weinberg and the Weinbergskirche.

Zimmerling epitomises the new generation which is pushing Sachsen wines back towards the position they enjoyed two centuries ago: among the best in Germany. During the 17th century the royal wine domaine played the leading role but today it is played by independent winegrowers who have built their estates from nothing.

Dry white wines make up almost the entire production of Sachsen's handful of top producers. In this northerly climate they might be expected to be rather thin and acidic, but Zimmerling's dry Riesling, Grauburgunder and Traminer regularly achieve 12 or more degrees of alcohol in good vintages and are fresh but never sharp. The granite soil gives them a strong minerally character which makes the Rieslings reminiscent of wines from the Wachau in Austria and the Traminer not unlike certain Alsatian wines, yet they retain an elegance all their own.

Dresden's other important vineyards lie on the other side of the city close to Radebeul. These are best reached by taking the Augustusbrücke from the town centre then following signs for Meissen. The most impressive buildings here are those of Schloss Wackerbarth which date from the late 1720s. They house Sachsen's State winery which cultivates one third of the region's vineyards but whose wines – not even those from the great Radebeuler Goldener Wagen vineyard – cannot be recommended at present.

The belvedere set among formal gardens amid extensive vineyards is a familiar landmark and other houses and towers which dot the precipitous terraced vineyards are no less impressive.

If Sachsen's wine culture is also beginning to blossom here, just as at Pillnitz, Meissen and Diesbar-Seuslitz, then it is because of private rather than State initiative. Although Radebeul's leading winemakers, Friedrich Aust and Klaus Seifert, currently have pitifully small areas of vineyards at their disposal they are already demonstrating what potential these vineyards possess. Müller-Thurgau yields sleek, racy wines with a pronounced minerally character unusual for this mundane grape and Traminer can achieve an astonishing opulence considering the northerly location.

Here as elsewhere in the region it was largely the efforts of winegrowing enthusiasts rather than professionals that enabled Radebeul's vineyards to be replanted during the latter part of the communist period. Slowly these vineyards are coming onto the market, presenting the existing mini-estates with the prospect of rapid growth during the next few years.

Given more vines to work with we can expect some exciting wines during the coming years. The problem facing Sachsen's leading winemakers is that demand could easily outstrip production, so that they may find increasing difficulty in allocating wine.

PLACES OF INTEREST

Dresden Museums
Gemäldegallerie Alte Mesiter
and Porzellansammlung
Zwinger, Theatreplatz
D 01067 Dresden
Tel : (0351) 4840120
An important collection of old masters including Rembrandts and paintings of the city by Canaletto. The porcelain collection of August the Strong is hardly less impressive. Closed Mondays.

Gemäldegalerie Neue Meister
und Grüner Gewölbe
Albertinum
Georg-Treu-Platz /
Brühlsche Terrasse
D 01067 Dresden
Tel: (0351) 4953056
Extensive collection of 19th- and 20th-century German art featuring a fine group of paintings by the Romantic Caspar David Friedrich. The Grüner Gewölbe remains here until restoration of the Schloss allows it to return to its traditional home. Closed Mondays.

Karl-May-Museum
Karl-May-Strasse 5
D 01445 Radebeul
Tel: (0351) 762727
The home of author Karl May in the suburb of Radebeul has been preserved exactly as he left it.

RECOMMENDED PRODUCERS

Lehmann
An der Weinstrasse 26
D 01612 Seusslitz
Tel: (035267) 236
Joachim Lehmann makes very clean,
fruity dry wines at this miniature
estate. The Weissburgunder,
Traminer and Riesling are the best.
Most are sold in the estate's
'Seusslitzer Weinstuben' which offers
traditional local cooking. There are
also five modestly priced simple
guest rooms.

*Far right Meissen seen from the
Burgberg. The town grew from the
12th-century around a fortified
strategic position crossing the Elbe.
Below Albrechtsburg castle, built
in the late-15th century overlooking
the River Elbe, was commissioned
by the Margrave Albert.*

MEISSEN AND THE ELBE VALLEY

Meissen is arguably the most beautiful wine town in all
Germany, completely unspoilt by ugly modern buildings or
the more obvious signs of tourism. It stands in the last narrow
stretch of the Elbe Valley before the river flows onto the plain
of the Sachsen Lowlands. To reach the town take the B6 from
the centre of Dresden. The first vineyard, the excellent
Kapitelberg, appears on the opposite bank of the river just
four kilometres before you reach the centre of town.

The ancient core of Meissen stands on the rocky
promontory of the Burgberg where the first castle was
erected by King Heinrich I in 929. The first bridge over
the river was constructed in the 13th century and the town
wall a century later. The Albrechtsburg, primarily in late-
Gothic style, has recently been extremely cautiously
restored and now appears as the perfect fairy-tale castle. Its
construction began in 1471 and was completed in 1525
with some Renaissance elements creeping in towards the
end of the work. It stood virtually empty for centuries: not
until August the Strong moved the royal porcelain factory
here in 1710 was it finally put to use. In 1863 Meissen
Porcelain moved to the Triebischtal at the bottom of the
hill and a massive renovation programme began in the

castle. During the course of the work a series of large neo-Gothic murals were painted and the vaulted ceilings decorated by 11 members of the Dresden art academy. The artists disregarded any consideration of historical accuracy but the extravagant works give the interior a dream-like quality. On October 3rd 1990, the Free State of Saxony was founded right here in the castle.

The Dom of Meissen with its twin spires is one of Germany's most beautiful Gothic cathedrals. Its rich collection of stone carvings and sculptures, most from the years shortly after construction was begun in 1260, merit lengthy study. Next to the cathedral is the Bishop's palace, another late-Gothic building dating from the late-15th century.

Alongside the great monuments of Miessen the area's leading wine producer, Dr Georg Prinz zur Lippe of the Schloss Proschwitz estate, has established a wine store where the wines from his and other private estates in the region can be tasted and bought. Meissen is also home to the region's cooperative whose 2,000 members account for roughly two-thirds of the region's production but

Schloss Proschwitz
D 01665 Proschwitz über Meissen
Tel: (03521) 452096
In 1991 Dr Georg Prinz zur Lippe bought back his family's wine estate which had been confiscated by the communists and proceeded to turn everything upside down. The dry Grauburgunders are now the best wines but all are clean and fresh. Appointment recommended; essential at weekends.

Jan Ulrich
Meissener Strasse 4
D 01612 Diesbar
Tel: (035267) 220
Jan Ulrich, only in his mid-20s, has built up this estate from scratch. More than half the production is dry Kerner, which is always fruity and well made, but the Riesling is best. Appointment essential at weekends.

RESTAURANTS

Merker's Weinstuben
Meissener Strasse 10
D 01612 Diesbar
Tel: (035267) 780
Albrecht Merker runs a charming
Weinstube on the bank of the Elbe
and serves honest country cooking
of a high standard. The selection of
wines from the region's best
producers (including good dry
Weissburgunder from his own
vineyards) is well priced. There are
also a few modestly priced, attractive
hotel rooms.

Vincenz Richter
An der Frauenkirche 12
D 01662 Meissen
Tel: (03521) 453285
This traditional restaurant housed
in Meissen's most beautiful half-
timbered house serves very good
regional cooking. The large wine list
includes a range from all Germany's
regions and a small international
selection. Modest prices. Reservation
essential in summer.

HOTELS

Lehmann
See Recommended Producers.
Merker's Weinstuben
See Restaurants.
Panonia Parkhotel
Hafenstrasse 27–31
D 01662 Meissen
Tel: (03521) 72250
The eccentric, brightly coloured tiled
façade of this most unusual hotel
immediately sets it apart from the
rest. Attractive, comfortable rooms
and some real style. Fair prices.

unfortunately, whilst it is possible to chance upon good
bottles here, there is little consistency in quality.

The main body of the town lies below the Burgbergand
as you wander among its labyrinthine streets every turn
seems to reveal a prospect more charming and fascinating
than the last. Some of the most imposing buildings lie
around the Markt where regular markets are still held.
They include the late-Gothic Frauenkirche with its
distinctive tower and the late-15th-century Rathaus from
the same period. Facing the town hall is the Renaissance
Apotheke or pharmacy of 1560 and several other
particularly impressive houses from the 15th–18th
centuries. Just around the corner is the renowned Vincenz
Richter wine restaurant in an almost impossibly
picturesque half-timbered house dating from 1523. Tucked
away in the backstreets is the former Augustine Foundation
of St Afra, the building a mix of Gothic and Renaissance
architecture. The porcelain factory's museum and display
rooms give a fascinating insight into the history of the
industry and the development of the region's culture.

Cross the Elbbrücke to the right bank of the Elbe to
reach the more modern part of town where there are some
magnificent late-19th century villas. Take the road which
follows the river downstream and at the edge of town the
first vineyards appear, clinging to narrow stony terraces.
These vineyards, the Katzensprung site of Meissen, surely
have the potential to yield remarkable wines. Their
southwesterly position right next to the river and their
porphyry soil is very similar to that of the top vineyards of

Right *A Renaissance pharmacy
(1560) overlooks Meissen's
marketplace.*

the Nahe and during the 18th century they were famous for giving some of the region's finest wines. Again the devastating effects of the pylloxera epidemic initiated a decline which subsequent economic crises and war could only accelerate. The Prinz zur Lippe's estate (signposted from here) is in nearby Proschwitz.

From the edge of Meissen it is a short drive to the charming wine villages of Diesbar and Seusslitz. They present the opposite extreme to the bustle of Dresden which, amongst the vineyards, woods and fields here, seems a million miles away. The most interesting producers are established master Joachim Lehmann and the relative newcomer to Sachsen's wine scene, Jan Ulrich.

The remains of Suesslitz' Gothic abbey church were incorporated in to the baroque Schloss of 1726 which stands at the northern edge of the village. Its formal gardens are in the French and English styles and the terraced vineyards surrounding them are crowned by the Heinrichsburg – not a medieval fortification as the name might suggest but an 18th-century garden house. From the 'Burg' there is a marvellous view of the whole complex. The Schloss is perfectly integrated into the landscape and gives an impression much more harmonious than the dominating grandeur typical of the period.

Some of the first vineyards in this area were planted during the 12th century (the oldest record dates from 1161 in Meissen). Hopefully it will not be long before wines like the 1783, described at the time as "delicate and precious", are once again produced from these vineyards.

Above *Vineyards close to Meissen where viticulture was first recorded in 1161.*

Below *The twin spires of the beautiful Gothic Dom rise above the castle. Built between the 13th and 15th centuries, the cathedral contains many priceless works of art.*

GLOSSARY

Anbaugebiet – literally 'region of origin'. Germany has 13 winegrowing regions

Auslese – traditionally rich, naturally sweet wine made from selected late picked grapes, but today the German wine law defines the category in purely analytic terms. Some of these wines are now vinified dry (see Trocken and Halbtrocken)

Autobahn – the German motorway. Still without tolls or speed limits (except where signs indicate otherwise!)

Bach – a small stream, sometimes incorporated in to vineyard names, eg the Goldbächel of Wachenheim/Pfalz

Bäckerei – a bakery, which in Germany means a source of real bread, an essential part of the survival kit for any wine tour

Barrique – small oak cask, most commonly of 225 or 300 litres of French or local wood used for the fermentation and/or maturation of red and white wines. Until recently German 'Barrique-Weine' were usually too oaky, but some fine examples are now being made

Beerenauslese – extremely rich, luscious wine produced from shrivelled, botrytis-affected berries (see Edelfäule). If made from Riesling or other noble grapes rare and expensive

Bundesstrasse – main highways, each of which has a number that appears on roadsigns. Unless indicated otherwise the speed limit is 100 kilometers per hour

Burg – a fortified tower or keep

Dom – a cathedral (see Münster)

Edelfäule – noble rot. Most of the great German dessert wines are produced from grapes affected by this fungus (*Botrytis cinerea*)

Edelstahl – stainless steel, the modern alternative to wood for the construction of wine casks

Eiswein – ice wine, made from grapes picked whilst frozen

Erzeugerabfüllung – literally 'bottled by the producer', which today usually means by a cooperative (see Gutsabfüllung and Winzergenossenschaft)

Federweisse – fermenting wine sold during the harvest period. Milky in appearance and yeasty in flavour it is traditionaly drunk with onion tart

Filtration – all German white wines are filtered before bottling, an essential operation to gaurantee their stability. Some top German reds are now bottled unfiltered

Fuder – the traditional 1,000 litre oak barrel used in the Mosel-Saar-Ruwer since Roman times

Gärung – fermentation, which in Germany can last anything from a few days to six months

Gutsabfüllung – estate-bottled (see Erzeugerabfüllung)

Halbtrocken – legal designation for wines that are just off dry. Depending on the grape and region these can either taste completely dry or quite sweet

Hectare (ha) – measure of area, approximately 2.47 acres

Hectolitre – measure of volume, 100 litres

Hefe(brand) – spirit distilled from the lees left after fermentation, usually water white and softer than Trester

Jahrgang – the vintage

Kabinett – traditionally the lightest German wines with alcohol levels that can go as low as 7 degrees in the Mosel-Saar-Ruwer, but law sadly sets no maximum alcohol limit

Keller – the cellar

Kellerei – a company which buys, blends and bottles wine, the equivalent of a *négociant* in France

Kelterhaus – the press house

Kirche – a church

Lage – an individual vineyard site or 'Einzellage'. Unfortunately the names of 'Grosslage', or collective sites which cover much larger areas, read like Einzellage names

Land – Germany is a federation of states , or 'Lände'. Not to be confused with Anbaugebiete, or winegrowing regions

Landwein – sub-category of Table Wine (see Tafelwein) for dry, normally cheap, quaffing wines

Lees – the dead yeast that settles to the bottom of the cask after fermentation

Lese – the harvest

Lieblich – designation for wines with natural sweetness that appears on price lists, but almost never on labels

Markt – a market or marketplace

Metzger – a butcher, often also selling ham and sausage (see Schinken and Wurst)

Most – freshly pressed grape juice

Münster – a minster, or cathedral

Oechsle – measure of the grape sugar content. The German wine law classifies the nation's wines solely on the basis of grape sugar content

Offene Weine – wines available in restaurants and bars to buy by the glass

Pfifferlinge – chanterelle mushrooms, an important speciality during the summer months

Qualitätswein (QbA) – legal designation for wines which have been chaptalized (ie to which sugar has been added during the fermentation to increase the alcoholic content)

Rathaus – the town hall

Säure – acidity, a vital consituent of German white wines. It is usually measured in gramms per litre of tartaric acid, but analytical figures are little guide to taste or quality

Schatzkammer – rarities, or library cellar

Schinken – ham, which may be cooked, dried or smoked

Schnitzel –a steak; unless the menu says otherwise it will almost certainly be pork. A cliché of German cooking

Schloss – usually translated as castle, but actually a palace rather than a set of fortifications

Schînung – fining, or the addition of substances to young wines to aid their clarification. Whilst France's top vintners prefer to fine rather than filter young wines, most of Germany's top quality wines are lightly filtered, but unfined

Sekt – sparkling wine

Spargel – asparagus, an important speciality during the months of April, May and June. In Germany, it is usually white and served as a main dish, accompanied by ham or a small steak

Spätlese – traditionally a late-harvested wine with some natural sweetness. Today the law sets disgracefully low minimum standards for this category, and only examples from reputable growers will be something special

Spitzenlage – a top vineyard site, today often referred to as 'Grand Cru'

Steillage – a steeply sloping vineyard site

Steinpilze – the German name for câpes or porcini mushrooms, an important speciality during the summer and early autumn

Stück – the oval, 1,200 litre casks used in the Rhine Valley since at least the Middle Ages

Sulphur dioxide – an antioxidant used in all wine; harmless, but sometimes detectable in very young wines

Tafelwein – Table Wine

Trester (brand) – the German name for marc or grappa, a spirit distilled from the grape skins left after pressing, often as rough as its foreign cousins

Trocken – the legal designation for dry wines

Trockenbeerenauslese – the pinnacle of Germany's legal wine classification system. Extremely rich, super-luscious wines made from raisin-like shrivelled berries. If made from Riesling or other noble grapes very rare and extremely expensive

Vietel(e) – a quarter litre glass of wine

Weinberg – a vineyard

Weingut – a wine estate

Winzergenossenschaft – a winemaking co-operative

Wurst – sausage, which comes in a thousand forms, cooked and cured

INDEX

Indexer's note: Names of
grape varieties and varietal
wines are indexed together
eg Müller-Thurgau grapes
and wines 12, 14, 27 where
12, 14 refers to the grape
variety and 27 to the wine
made from it. Towns are
given in brackets for hotels
and restaurants.

129

GAZETTEER

PICTURE CREDITS